The Teacher Chronicles

Confronting the Demands of Students, Parents, Administrators and Society

By Natalie Schwartz

Laurelton
MEDIA

The Teacher Chronicles
Confronting the Demands of Students, Parents, Administrators and Society

By Natalie Schwartz

P.O. Box 660
Millwood, New York 10546
www.laureltonmedia.com

Editor: Carl Mercurio
Copyeditor: Amy Borrelli
Proofreader: Linda Kopp
Editorial Consultant: Matthew Howe
Editorial Consultant: Jennifer Martz
Editorial Consultant: Melissa Tammaro
Marketing Consultant: Liz Greene
Layout Editor: Laura Wurzel
Cover Photo: Peter Mariuzza

Printed in the United States of America

Library of Congress Control Number: 2008928054

ISBN: 978-0-9816935-0-7

Table of Contents

Foreword

By David McCullagh

Board of Education Member, New York

In my many years as a school board member and as a parent, I have learned that there are few things that arouse more passion, interest, concern and sometimes fury than the education of our children. From the exciting and nerve-wracking first day of preschool or kindergarten through high school graduation day, our children are entrusted to schools for about seven hours a day to receive a large share of their education and socialization. We have a name for those who are brave (and some might say foolish) enough to take on this awesome responsibility—we call them teachers.

The teaching profession is one of life's great paradoxes.

It is at the same time one of the most familiar jobs there is and also perhaps one of the most misunderstood. Most adults have attended more than a dozen years of school and perhaps have relived the experience many times over through their children. The erroneous notion that many people possess is that they have seen hundreds of teachers in action over the course of their lives, so there could not be anything about the teaching profession that they do not know. The truth, it turns out, is not that simple, and this book eloquently clears up many of those misconceptions.

One of the many things that *The Teacher Chronicles* does exceptionally well is to challenge the notion of how much we really know about the people who educate our children. The book does this by offering insights into how teaching and education have evolved over the years. To fully describe how education has changed since most parents attended school as students would be the subject of a rather lengthy book in its own right. One of the most important myths that this book debunks is the notion that teaching is a nine-to-three job, with summers off. Teachers face new demands on many fronts that impact the amount of time required to fulfill their responsibilities. The immediacy of today's forms of communication, such as e-mail, voice mail and cell phones, raises the bar in terms of expectations of teacher-parent communication and can add hours to the workday. Other demands that impact a teacher's day and summer schedule include teaching to new, high-stakes testing requirements brought about through No Child Left Behind (NCLB) legislation; teaching to the diverse learning styles of special needs students that are increasingly brought into mainstream classrooms through inclusion and collaborative learning initiatives; fulfilling professional development requirements that often must be done in the summer months due to time constraints during the school year; the list is endless.

It is the stories, told by the teachers from their point of view, that give this book its voice and power. The author has done her homework and has interviewed more than 50 teachers from all over the country, across all grades and disciplines, to give the reader a true sense of what the job of teaching is like. She does not get in the way of the stories at all and only interjects occasionally with timely data and information to give the reader a deeper understanding of the subject.

So why should someone read *The Teacher Chronicles?* The stories about today's students and parents are at the very least fascinating and at the most shocking. Stories about students intentionally getting a teacher they do not like in trouble are disturbing yet compelling reading. The stories about the lengths some parents will go to to help their children with grades, socialization and the all-important college acceptance raise concerns about how our society has perverted the meaning of a good education. One thing that no one will challenge after reading the book is that students and parents are much savvier about their rights than previous generations, and they are not afraid to bully teachers to get their way. This phenomenon takes its toll on many teachers and is a big reason many potentially great instructors decide to leave the profession for less demanding jobs.

The book, however, does not center on titillating stories that show the education system at its worst. Rather, the bulk of the stories that the teachers relate provide great insights into what it takes to be a successful teacher in light of today's *new* challenges (no one denies that challenges in the profession have always existed). *The Teacher Chronicles* at its heart reveals the passion, the caring, and the commitment that all great teachers need to have in common to be successful at their jobs. The theme and common thread that unites most of the stories in the book is that the ability to reach those students who are at risk and inspire them to learn and achieve is what makes teaching such a rewarding profession. Most teachers are more than willing to put up with the challenges of their profession to make a difference in the lives of children.

So who would benefit from reading *The Teacher Chronicles?* The most obvious audience is teachers. By reading this book, new teachers will receive a roadmap for success and will hopefully be able to avoid the common pitfalls that bedevil many inexperienced teachers. Experienced teachers will perhaps relate best to the "war stories" about their profession, and the book will help them connect with why they chose to be teachers in the first place. Parents who read *The Teacher Chronicles* will gain a better understanding of their child's teacher, as well as the parent's role in the education process. The book points out that "parental involvement in a child's education is a major factor in determining academic success" (page 74). A successful relationship among all parties is the classic "three-legged stool," where students, teachers and parents understand the role each plays in the process, and respect and value the contributions of the others involved. Another important group that would benefit from reading this book is taxpayers. Our public schools have the only governmental budgets that citizens have the power to say "yes" or "no" to each year. Many citizens vent their frustrations with high taxes in general by voting "no" to school budgets. This book will show taxpayers how the education system has evolved to meet the needs of diverse learners and how hard teachers work to make a difference in the lives of our children. Reading *The Teacher Chronicles* will help our citizens make more informed decisions when they go to the polls to vote on their school budgets each year.

Teachers help provide students with the skills, knowledge and attitudes they need to be successful in whatever fields they decide to pursue. Really great teachers inspire our children to want to learn more, to spend the rest of their lives satisfying their own sense of curiosity and pursuing knowledge for its own sake. *The Teacher Chronicles* tells the story of these remarkable people, and tells it in their own words. We all owe it to them to sit back and listen. Who knows, we may learn something.

Chapter One

Introduction–
Confronting the Demands

When Kim Thompson arrived at a New York City elementary school on her first day as a new teacher in the mid-1990s, she was greeted by a chalk outline of a dead body in front of the school building. She glanced across the parking lot, which was littered with shattered beer bottles, crack vials and condoms, and noticed another rundown elementary school with a tattered American flag dangling pathetically in front. The scene heralded an emotionally intense, mentally draining and physically exhausting year.

After entering the building, Ms. Thompson headed to the main office to call her husband. She wanted to let him know she arrived safely at the school. A member of the office staff instructed her to use a pay phone because the school district refused to pay for personal calls. But the office did keep a spare battery on hand in case the nearby chop shop stripped a teacher's car. She remembers teachers going there to buy back their car parts. She also recalls a memo that was distributed advising teachers not to stand in front of the windows to avoid stray bullets.

The school provided Ms. Thompson with a few books for her first grade class—not enough to go around—and some paper. She had to purchase the rest of the books, teaching materials and supplies with her own money. Her salary was about $28,000, but she shelled out about $8,000 for the instructional materials and supplies that she needed to teach her class. She purchased a rug for some of the students to sit on because her classroom did not have enough chairs and desks. The space was even more cramped when another class had to join hers because a teacher was absent.

She had 30 students in her class, about two-thirds of whom should have been placed in a special education class that could better meet their needs. Not only was she ill-equipped to instruct children with special needs, but she was also unprepared to deal with the emotional and physical needs of the rest of the class. One child's shoes were so old and torn that Ms. Thompson bought her a new pair of sneakers. She bought another child a doll. At breakfast and lunch time she watched as the students turned their trays upside down and tapped them to release every crumb because they were starving. The meals they received at the school were often the only regular meals they had. She provided dinner for one of her students regularly because she was concerned the child was not eating enough. She worried about her students during vacations because they didn't have access to the school meal program. One of the students was losing her hair due to lack of nutrition.

While worrying about the well-being of 30 children was emotionally taxing, Ms. Thompson's frustration with the principal's academic policies took the greatest mental toll. The school's principal advocated the "whole language" method of reading instruction, which involves teaching students to remember entire words. However, the students were not progressing through this tactic; Ms. Thompson felt they would respond better to phonics, which entails teaching students to sound out words. However, the principal would not allow her to utilize this method. By the end of the year, only two of her 30 students could read, causing Ms. Thompson to feel like she failed them.

Despite the difficulties she encountered at the school, she stayed due to her sense of responsibility. "I felt like I had made a commitment to the kids and I had to go," she says. She had friends who left their teaching jobs at the school after only three weeks. But she felt compelled to stay for the remainder of the school year. The children were sweet and they needed her. She felt like a mother to them. But her professional differences with the school principal made it impossible for her to do her job. She did not return to the school the following year. (Ms. Thompson's experiences at her next job are discussed in Chapter 4.)

Across the country in an affluent California community, Cynthia Collins has faced a different set of challenges at the middle school where she teaches. The year she was pregnant, one of her students tried to have her fired. The day she found out she was carrying a girl, she announced the news to her class and handed out pink candy. One of the boys in her class wrote a letter to the administration, complaining that he found it offensive that she discussed her pregnancy. The student also asserted that Ms. Collins did not deserve her position at the school.

She was devastated. She feared she would lose her job because she didn't have tenure yet. Although she retained her job, the student remained in her class and continued to torment her. She was forced to tolerate his abuse while she endured a difficult pregnancy. The student made hostile comments to her. When her protruding belly accidentally brushed against him, he told her to "get that away from me." And he taunted her. After presenting her with flowers, he made an obscene gesture when he thought she had turned away.

"That is one kid I can say I hate," she says. "But at least I can say by June, he's gone. He really scared me. He was evil." Throughout the ordeal, she tried to focus on the positive. Her students threw her two baby showers, and parent volunteers in the class were always supportive, showering her with hugs and bringing her water.

Ms. Collins has also faced conflicts with parents. One student's father sent her a belligerent e-mail message. The boy repeatedly and aggressively harassed his friend; Ms. Collins felt compelled to intervene. She had a talk with the victim, and advised him that the bully was not acting like much of a friend. She also called the victim's parents, who told the bully's parents about the phone call they received from her. The father of the bully reacted by sending Ms. Collins the hostile e-mail message. The e-mail was sent at 4:30 a.m. and barked, "What the hell do you think you're doing?" The father accused Ms. Collins of trying to destroy his son's friendships. Both boys denied Ms. Collins' claims.

The bully continued to harass the other students in the class. One of his victims was afflicted with scoliosis. The bully slapped the boy so hard he lost his balance and collapsed onto the ground. Ms. Collins reported the incident to the parents and the administration, but the victim denied it happened and the bully faced no consequences. While frustrated by the episode, she consoles herself with the knowledge that she did the right thing by trying to protect her student.

When Ms. Collins struggles with distressing situations, she reminds herself that the enjoyable and rewarding aspects of her job outweigh the frustrating ones. (More details about Ms. Collins' experiences appear in Chapter 4.)

* * *

Most Americans have experienced the public school system as students, and some have journeyed through it a second time as parents. But they have not experienced the system from the inside, from the teacher's point of view. In an effort to understand their perspective, I set out to interview teachers around the country. I started with teachers I knew, who referred me to other teachers. I asked my friends to put me in touch with teachers they knew, who connected me with other teachers. I focused on regular education classroom teachers in public schools, grades K to 12, but I also spoke with a few specialists, private school teachers and special education teachers. Eventually, I spoke with more than 50 teachers. This book contains their stories.

I protected the identities of the teachers who agreed to interviews by changing their names and referring only to the states where they teach. I chose to omit their names and school districts to encourage them to speak honestly without fear of repercussions from the parents, administrators and school boards for whom they work. Protecting their identities also eliminated their motivation to portray themselves in a positive light.

The process I went through to find teachers to interview yielded a random selection of participants. I did not seek out teachers who are prominent due to their successes or teachers who are infamous because of their transgressions. These are not the stories covered in newspaper articles or portrayed in movies. They do not reflect the extremes, but rather the day-to-day experiences of America's teachers. And those daily experiences range from challenging and stressful to outrageous and shocking. Taken together, they reveal the underlying complexities of the teaching profession.

The reader should bear in mind that my goal was to uncover the challenges and demands teachers face. I did not focus on the positive and rewarding aspects of the profession, which have already been covered thoroughly in film and literature. However, most of the teachers profiled have a positive attitude toward their jobs and find teaching exciting and fulfilling, despite the challenges they face.

The reader should also keep in mind that the information contained in these pages is not intended to excuse teachers who fail their students and disappoint parents. But regardless of whether a teacher is considered successful or deemed unsuccessful, they all have to deal with the same challenges. The information in this book conveys those challenges. Certainly some teachers are more adept than others at handling them.

The quality of a teacher's experience varies from year to year, depending on the students, parents and administrators he or she deals with. A teacher may have a class full of students with behavior problems one year and a group of model students the next. If a principal who is a trusted and supportive mentor resigns and is replaced by a principal with a completely different managerial style, the teacher's experience is dramatically altered. A teacher may work with respectful and supportive parents one year, and uncooperative and difficult parents the next.

* * *

While teachers are well-trained for the academic aspect of their jobs, they are often unprepared to handle students' emotional and behavioral issues or unsupportive parents, according to Linda Barrett, a professor of teacher education at a college in New York.

Teachers deal with different issues depending on their locations, Dr. Barrett says. In general, teachers in lower socio-economic areas are often dealing with classroom management issues and a lack of parental involvement. In higher socio-economic areas, parents are heavily involved and school districts demand teachers produce high scores on state assessment tests. Regardless of their locations, teachers say one of the most challenging aspects of the profession is that they are accountable to so many groups of interested parties—students, parents, administrators, school boards, taxpayers, and even the state and federal government.

"You're responsible to a lot of stakeholders," says Helen Lewis, a

New York City middle school teacher. But the most difficult part of the job is working with children. "The kids are your consumers, and they don't necessarily buy your product every day," says Ms. Lewis, who used to take jobs during the summer in the private sector. "Any time I've worked in an exclusively adult environment, it's a cake walk," she says. "Kids will test you in ways adults won't." A colleague in the corporate world may pursue advancement at your expense or engage in a power struggle, but you usually know what to expect from another adult, she says. "Kids bring anything from A to Z."

Dr. Barrett shares her experiences as an inner-city teacher to help prepare her students for the more unsettling and surprising aspects of the job. She tells them about the time a parent struck one of her colleagues over the head with a baseball bat and how her car was broken into and her battery was stolen. But most teachers agree that there is no way to fully prepare for the job. Knowledge, confidence and efficiency come with experience.

* * *

Synopsis of the Teacher Interviews

Who Are the Teachers Profiled?

◆ **They teach throughout the country.**

The teachers profiled in this book work in California, Colorado, Connecticut, Florida, Georgia, Massachusetts, Missouri, Nevada, New Jersey, New York, South Carolina, Ohio and Tennessee.

- **They teach in a variety of socio-economic settings.**

  Their school districts are in inner cities, middle class suburbs, affluent metropolitan areas and rural communities.

- **They embarked on diverse paths.**

  Many of the teachers profiled attained their teaching certification in college and became teachers immediately after graduation. Some of them pursued careers in other fields—such as retail and information technology—before deciding to become teachers. A few engaged in volunteer work or joined the armed forces before becoming teachers.

- **They have different levels of experience.**

  One of the teachers profiled is in her first year and one has been teaching for five decades. The rest fall somewhere in between. Most are still teachers, but a few have left the profession to raise families or to pursue other careers. A couple of them are retired.

Why Did They Become Teachers?

- **They love learning.**
- **They enjoy working with children.**
- **They had inspirational teachers when they were students.**
- **Their parents were teachers.**

What Are the Major Challenges They Face?

- **Classroom Management**

Disruptive behavior in the classroom distracts the other students and interferes with the teacher's ability to maintain the attention of the class. At the elementary school level, teachers often have to deal with noisy, unruly or even physically aggressive students. At the middle school and high school levels, teachers may have difficulty maintaining control of the classroom because they do not command respect from their students. (Classroom management is covered in Chapter 2.)

♦ **Cultivating successful relationships with parents.**

Teachers believe children benefit most when teachers and parents develop constructive relationships, and they approach the child's education as a team. Building such a relationship with 20 to 150 parents—depending on the grade level—is an arduous task, but a critical one. In cases where parents don't value the teacher's input or trust the teacher's ability to determine their child's academic needs and abilities, the task becomes more difficult. When parents approach teachers with an adversarial attitude such as this, the teacher faces obstacles to fostering the child's academic progress. The barriers to success are just as high when parents are detached from the classroom and uninvolved in their child's education. (The parent-teacher relationship is covered in Chapter 3.)

♦ **Navigating school district politics.**

Teachers are under pressure to please students, parents, administrators, school boards, and state and federal education departments. Most teachers agree that these interested parties are justified in having high expectations of teachers, and they strive to meet the demands placed on them. But the pressure can be overwhelming. When parents are uncooperative, and administrators and colleagues unsupportive, the pressure becomes even more intense. (School politics is covered in Chapter 4.)

◆ **Dealing with the emotional needs of students.**

Teachers are more than just educators. They are guidance counselors, therapists, caregivers and more. Teachers in lower socio-economic areas often purchase school supplies, food and clothing for their students. When a student is facing a personal crisis, the teacher is often the one to pick up on it and help the student deal with it. Attempting to care for, help and support so many children can be emotionally draining and mentally taxing for teachers. In addition to the mental and emotional burdens of the job, teachers less frequently find themselves in physical danger when a student becomes violent. (The mental and physical hazards teachers face are covered in Chapter 5.)

◆ **Managing a heavy workload and busy schedule with no downtime.**

Contrary to the pervasive belief that teachers work until 3 p.m., most teachers work after school and on weekends to prepare lessons, grade papers and communicate with parents. Because they spend most of their days teaching students, they have limited time to handle these tasks during the school day. Free periods are quickly consumed by a variety of tasks. While the advent of e-mail, voice mail and cell phones has improved parent-teacher communication—an important factor in student success—the over-use of these forms of communication can create unrealistic expectations of teachers. Due to e-mail and voice mail, parents expect that teachers can immediately address their questions and concerns. (The teacher's workload and hours are covered in Chapter 6.)

What Makes Teachers Successful?

- **They possess inherent personality traits that make them natural-born educators.**
- **They demonstrate the ability to handle all of the facets of the job.**
- **They find ways to manage difficult situations.**
- **They find ways to cope with the stress associated with their jobs.**
- **They find their jobs exciting and rewarding, despite the challenges they face.**

* * *

Most teachers do not resent the pressures that are thrust upon them; they accept them as part of the job. And they heartily embrace and enjoy their jobs despite these pressures. However, they acknowledge that the lack of respect and financial compensation they receive is distressing.

I did not intend this book to be a commentary on the American education system or the government's policies. My goal, in part, was to provide teachers with a compilation of stories to which they can relate. But I also had a broader objective in mind. Teachers are responsible for the safety and welfare of our children for six hours or more each day, and they are entrusted with the vital task of educating the future leaders of America. I wanted to gain a better understanding of the pressures and demands they face and how they perceive their jobs. I hope others will share my interest.

Chapter Two

The Classroom Management Struggle

"If a child is totally disruptive and running around, it's impossible to teach."

Susan Johnson, Middle School Teacher, Tennessee

Behavior Issues

Kate Adams, Elementary School Teacher, New York

Kate Adams has always enjoyed working with children. She read to kindergarten classes when she was an elementary school student. In high school, she participated in the Junior Achievement program, which encourages business leaders and high school students to go into classrooms and teach a variety of lessons, from operating a donut factory to learning about money and saving. During college she worked at an activity and fun center for children ages three and up. She also worked at Baby Gap, a children's clothing chain. She has a great appreciation for the attitude children have toward learning and their insatiable thirst for knowledge. "They are so open and willing to learn," she says.

When she graduated from college, Ms. Adams was ecstatic to receive a job offer to teach pre-K at an urban public school in New York State. The assistant principal who hired her was previously the assistant principal at the high school she attended. Her excitement evaporated quickly.

"Every day I was crying because I realized my education didn't really prepare me for the actual working experience," she says. She discovered that the knowledge she needed to be a teacher was not attainable from a college professor or from a textbook. Looking back on her first year, she says the confidence and skills required to be an effective teacher can be gained only through experience. But she also believes that the ability to develop the skills that successful teachers possess is innate in some individuals who pursue the profession, but not in all of them. "You have it or you don't," she says.

That first year, she was overwhelmed by the magnitude of her responsibility. She had 20 children in her class, and she felt solely accountable for the welfare, the academic progress, and the social development of each one of them. "At Baby Gap, I was responsible for the denim," she says.

Throughout the year she found herself filling a variety of roles that she was not prepared for—psychologist, guidance counselor, nurse, among a host of others. Her difficulties can be attributed, in part, to her inexperience. But she also had to contend with a particularly challenging group of children. She was so overwhelmed by the job the first few weeks that she walked into her assistant principal's office, thanked him for the opportunity, and dropped her keys on his desk, signifying her intention to resign. She did not want to quit. The gesture was a plea for help. She told the assistant principal she was not cut out for the job or she was doing something wrong. She doubted her ability to handle the job she had always wanted to do.

One of her students had a difficult home life and acted out in class. She would stand on the table, bark at the students and staff, lash out violently, and roll back and forth on the floor, bumping into the other kids. She bit one of the teaching assistants and hit the other students. Ms. Adams says she was so stunned by the student's behavior she didn't know what to do or how to help her. She had studied behavior modification plans in college, but this child's behavior was so severe that the measures she learned about did not seem to apply. She wound up holding the student's hand practically the whole day to keep her calm and restrain her from harming the other students. The student respected Ms. Adams and never became violent with her.

Another student in the class was not accustomed to being told "no" at home. Every time Ms. Adams told him he was not allowed to do something, he would cry. He misbehaved every day, and every day Ms. Adams' reaction caused him to cry. Another child with behavior issues pulled his pants down and exposed his buttocks to the music teacher. Yet another student left the class on the third day of school to run around in the gym; Ms. Adams tore through the school building frantically searching for him.

"As a first-year teacher, I didn't want to be super strict. It's not my personality," she says. She was exasperated, but didn't know how to handle the discipline problems in her class.

Also due to her lack of experience, she initiated activities that created more problems. She allowed the children to paint on the first day of school (while wearing their brand new clothing) before she had an opportunity to teach them how to use paint properly and request they bring smocks to school.

Because she was teaching a newly added pre-K section, her room was sparsely furnished and lacked a carpet and supplies. Supplies had been ordered but had not arrived. She was hired only days before the school year began and found herself scrambling to purchase items to decorate and outfit her room before the first day of school. She was concerned about making a good impression at parent orientation, and she knew the appearance of her room would make a negative impact if she did not spruce it up.

Her disillusionment caused her to avoid anything related to children outside of school. She used to love watching the television program, "Kids Say the Darndest Things." Her interest in watching the show vanished.

She relied on the support she received from her family, who encouraged her to persevere. She went to the bookstore every weekend to purchase books on helping children with behavior issues. She received guidance from her assistant principal, who would check in with her regularly to help her evaluate the methods that worked, those that didn't and the reasons why. She confided in colleagues with more experience, who dispensed advice and offered support.

She pushed herself to endure each day; the days turned into weeks, and the weeks into months. She realized her efforts were helping the children learn social skills, acquire academic concepts and modify their behavior. The main reason she made it through her first year was the progress of her students and the positive feedback she received from parents, many of whom told her their children loved coming to school.

Toward the end of the year, even after her situation was improving and her confidence was growing, she enrolled in a crisis intervention class to better prepare herself for dealing with difficult students. But none of her classes since her first year have been as difficult.

Ms. Adams taught the pre-K class for only one year before she was moved into a position teaching a multicultural "special" for kindergarten through fifth grade. (A special is a subject children take outside of the regular classroom, such as art, gym or music.) She taught the course for two years before accepting a reading enrichment program position, which primarily required her to prepare fourth graders for the ELA (New York's English-Language Arts exam). She held the position for two years. She has been teaching kindergarten for the past five years.

Over the years, she has faced issues with parents. During parent orientation one year, two parents started arguing with each other in the middle of her presentation because their children had a confrontation earlier in the day. She has had difficulty getting some parents involved in their children's education because they had negative experiences in school and don't necessarily trust teachers. On the opposite end of the spectrum, she has confronted parents who are overbearing. One mother insisted on meeting with Ms. Adams to discuss her child's report card. She demanded Ms. Adams explain every single grade on the report card. The woman became defensive and combative. But the next day, she gave Ms. Adams a box of chocolates and apologized for her behavior, blaming it on her menstrual cycle. (Issues concerning parents are covered in greater detail in Chapter 3.)

Ms. Adams says she tries to make a lasting impression on her students by giving them knowledge that transcends academics. She hopes to teach them to be caring and respectful people. She makes an effort to get to know each student in her class, to learn about their interests and to treat them as individuals. She tries to convey to all of her students that they are important and she cares about them. She makes time to listen to her students when they have something to say. "From 8:30 to 3:30, they are my children," she says.

But even after dismissal at 3:30 p.m., her students remain in her thoughts. She worries about them, particularly those who have difficult home lives. She is familiar with their backgrounds because she visits some of their homes for parent conferences.

She thinks about work all the time. When shopping for personal items, she finds herself straying from her original plans to search for books to buy for her class.

Yet her experience has made her more confident and more efficient. She recently became a mother and makes an effort to leave work at 3:30 p.m. each day. She works through her lunch period and all of her prep periods to avoid staying late at work. But the lack of downtime during the day is exhausting. She barely has time to use the bathroom, let alone check e-mail like many people with regular office jobs do to take a break. For her, there is no time for a break. She uses her summer vacation to decompress and rejuvenate. She knows that in September she must face the challenge of getting to know 20 new children and developing relationships with them and their parents. She knows she's accountable for preparing them thoroughly for first grade. And she's never satisfied with using the same instructional program year after year; she always enhances it with something new and different.

But when she has a good day, when all of the kids are on target, it's gratifying. She enjoys the constant challenge of teaching. If something she tries doesn't work, she strives to determine a solution so she can learn and grow professionally every year.

* * *

Teachers say classroom management is a critical aspect of their jobs. To teach effectively, teachers must minimize distractions and ensure students are focused and ready to learn. A child who is behaving improperly is not focused on the lesson or activity, and serves as a distraction for the rest of the class.

But classroom management extends beyond reining in poor behavior that can be disruptive to the classroom environment. Teachers must also address the needs of children with emotional and mental health issues to ensure they are receptive learners. The teacher must assuage a child who becomes consumed with anxiety because he or she doesn't understand a concept. The teacher must refocus the attention of a student with attention deficit hyperactivity disorder (ADHD) who becomes distracted during a lesson. If a child's improper behavior problem stems from an underlying emotional issue or mental disorder, the teacher must take this into consideration when determining the appropriate discipline.

An estimated 14% to 20% of children suffer some type of mental health problem, according to the Substance Abuse and Mental Health Services Administration (SAMHSA), an agency of the U.S. Department of Health and Human Services. Research suggests a variety of factors contribute to a child's emotional problems, including genetics, trauma and stress. While poor parenting or abuse can lead to emotional problems, more often parents and family are a child's greatest source of emotional support, according to SAMHSA. Regardless of the underlying causes, teachers face the overwhelming responsibility of dealing with a range of behavioral and emotional issues in the classroom.

Childhood and Adolescent Mental, Emotional and Behavioral Disorders

♦ **Anxiety Disorders:** Excessive fear, worry or uneasiness may be symptoms of anxiety disorders. As many as 13 out of every 100 children from ages nine to 17 have an anxiety disorder, according to one study. According to the Anxiety Disorders Association of America, children may suffer from the following anxiety disorders: panic disorder, social anxiety disorder, generalized anxiety disorder, specific phobias and separation anxiety disorder.

♦ **Attention Deficit Hyperactivity Disorder:** Children with ADHD have difficulty focusing their attention, are often impulsive, and are easily distracted. Most children with ADHD have difficulty remaining still, taking turns and staying quiet. According to the National Institute of Mental Health (NIMH), an estimated 3% to 5% of children, or about 2 million, have ADHD. Thus in a classroom of 25 to 30 students, it is likely that at least one will have the condition, the NIMH says.

♦ **Autism:** Children with autism have difficulty interacting and communicating with others. Symptoms range from mild to severe.

♦ **Bipolar Disorder:** Children and adolescents who have bipolar disorder or manic depression demonstrate exaggerated mood swings ranging from extreme highs to extreme lows.

♦ **Conduct Disorder:** Children who demonstrate a lack of regard for others and repeatedly violate the basic rights of others and the rules of society may suffer from conduct disorder.

Conduct disorder causes children to express their feelings and impulses in destructive ways.

◆ **Depression:** Two out of every 100 children may have major depression, and eight out of every 100 adolescents may suffer from the disease, according to studies. Children who suffer from depression feel sad or worthless, lose interest in activities, and experience a decline in school performance.

◆ **Eating Disorders:** Children or adolescents who fear gaining weight and do not believe they are underweight may have an eating disorder.

◆ **Learning Disorders:** Difficulties receiving or expressing information may indicate a learning disorder.

◆ **Oppositional Defiant Disorder:** Oppositional defiant disorder (ODD) is a pattern of disobedient, hostile and defiant behavior toward authority figures, according to the American Academy of Child & Adolescent Psychiatry. The behavior typically starts by eight years old. Children with ODD are often stubborn, have temper outbursts, become belligerent, argue with adults and refuse to obey. Some studies indicate that 20% of the school-age population is affected by ODD.

◆ **Schizophrenia:** Schizophrenia causes young people to have psychotic periods that may involve hallucinations, withdrawal from others and detachment from reality.

Sources: Substance Abuse and Mental Health Services Administration (SAMHSA), National Institute of Mental Health, Anxiety Disorders Association of America, American Academy of Child & Adolescent Psychiatry.

Even children who do not have specific emotional issues or behavior problems often require special attention at times, particularly in kindergarten and first grade. Many young children lack the level of independence required to take care of themselves for the entire school day. They rely on their teachers for support and assistance with any problem that arises, whether it's a stomachache, an unkind classmate or an untied shoelace. Thus the teacher is thrust into a surrogate parent role for 20 to 30 children.

* * *

Richard Bennett, Elementary School Teacher, South Carolina

After graduating from college, Richard Bennett spent more than three years as an officer in the Navy before pursuing a master's degree in education. "I always had a love of learning and reading," Mr. Bennett says of his decision to become a teacher. He also enjoyed working with children as a Boy Scouts camp counselor.

Mr. Bennett was hired as a second grade teacher at a New York City elementary school the day before school started. New to the school system and to teaching, he worked from 4 a.m. until 7 p.m. to catch up on lesson planning. In the evening, he passed out at 8 p.m. from exhaustion and resumed work the next day at 4 a.m. "It was brutal," he says. The stress and long hours he endured in the first four months on the job caused him to shed 30 pounds.

Of the 30 students in his class, three had severe emotional issues. One of his students faced a family environment that was shattered by domestic violence. "The girl couldn't cope with what was happening anywhere in her life, much less a classroom," he says. "By no means was she the only one in distress."

In addition to the children with severe emotional issues, Mr. Bennett had about five or six students who exhibited more typical behavior problems. He witnessed "off-the-wall" antics that pierced the solemnity of the classroom environment. One student had an affinity for climbing onto a desk and dancing. Attempting to teach a class in which a third of the students required special attention or constant discipline led to frustration and stress. The building administration tried to respond to the issues Mr. Bennett faced, but they were just as overwhelmed.

Mr. Bennett's youthful energy and stamina enabled him to cope with the stress and anxiety. He also found it helpful to consult with other teachers who faced similar situations. He enjoyed teaching the "amazingly sweet, nice kids" he had in his class, which helped mitigate the anguish of dealing with the more difficult students.

After two years, Mr. Bennett moved to South Carolina and accepted a position teaching third grade in a low-income rural district, where he continued to face behavior problems. After two years in South Carolina, he left the teaching profession to pursue a new career.

But it was not student behavior that ultimately prompted Mr. Bennett to give up teaching.

"The main reason I left was the parents had unrealistic expectations of what the teacher's role was," he says.

He felt that the parents did not understand and embrace the responsibilities associated with raising their children. Parents expected teachers to assume responsibility for teaching life skills, such as exhibiting proper behavior, understanding the difference between right and wrong, and appreciating the value of education. He believes that life skills and discipline must originate in the home, with parents setting and communicating high expectations.

To illustrate his point, Mr. Bennett cites an experience a friend of his had at a department store. The friend was on the check-out line behind a child who was misbehaving. The child's mother turned to the cashier and said, "What are they teaching these kids in school?" The anecdote demonstrates that even when a child is not in the school environment, the parent is inclined to blame the child's behavior on his or her teachers.

While the overwhelming expectations of parents caused Mr. Bennett's discontent to escalate during the two years he taught in South Carolina, a single episode led to his decision to leave the profession. The mother of one of his students contacted him to schedule a conference to discuss her child. The student was not behaving properly and was not performing well. "I don't know what she came in wanting to accomplish," he says. "She assaulted me." When she began pushing him, he called for the principal and assistant principal to come in, and they removed the woman from the room. The principal and assistant principal asked him not to press charges, which exacerbated his anguish over the incident. He left at the end of that school year.

Frustration with the parents and a lack of support from the administration were the major factors that caused Mr. Bennett to quit. But the compensation was also an issue. He was recently married and wanted to start a family.

"I enjoyed working with the students," he says. But in the end, that wasn't enough. "In many ways it's a pity because there are so few male teachers at the elementary school level."

Mr. Bennett believes that society's impression of teachers as altruistic mentors has led to the lack of support and compensation they receive. "People say it's a calling. It's ludicrous," he says. The belief that teachers have a passion for their job creates justification for saddling them with unrealistic demands and meager compensation, he says.

When Mr. Bennett left his teaching position, he enrolled in a training program offered by a local software company and learned to be a computer programmer. He has worked as a software engineer for the past 10 years.

* * *

Susan Johnson, Middle School Teacher, Tennessee

Susan Johnson, a retired middle school teacher in rural Tennessee, had as many as 40 students in her class in the late 1970s. By the 1980s, class size had dwindled to between 20 and 35, still a sizeable group. Managing a class of 30 to 40 students, all of whom have different needs and skill levels, is a daunting task, she says. But responding effectively to children with special needs in a large classroom environment is particularly challenging.

Federal and state law requires schools to place children with special needs in the "least restrictive environment" possible, a regulation that is a "double-edged sword," she says. The regular classroom can be a positive environment for children with special needs. But if the child has behavior issues that the teacher is unable to handle, it can create an environment that is not conducive to learning.

"If a child is totally disruptive and running around, it's impossible to teach," Ms. Johnson says. Sometimes the child's behavior stems from emotional distress, and the teacher has to find a way to reach the child to modify his or her behavior. In her seventh and eighth grade math class in the early 1980s, she had a student who saw his father kill his mother. He had a short temper, and was easily provoked into fights by his classmates. If his teacher had to leave the classroom, a fight would typically ensue. His classmates took turns getting him into trouble.

Ms. Johnson avoided leaving him in the classroom with the other children by pretending she needed a "bodyguard" and assigning him the job. Whenever she left the classroom, she asked him to join her to protect her. If she went to the bathroom, he would sit outside the door. "You have to have a mechanism to protect the children from themselves," she says.

She had another student in her seventh grade math class who would urinate in her pants whenever she got upset. Ms. Johnson found that putting her hand on the girl's shoulder to calm her down had a soothing effect.

In addition to dealing with emotionally troubled children, Ms. Johnson faced obstacles to motivating her students to strive for success in school. The parents of many of her students had negative experiences in school and did not graduate from high school. They did not convey the value of education to their children. She felt compelled to ensure her students had positive experiences.

Ms. Johnson believes in a dual-track education system, beginning in sixth grade, that provides vocational training as well as academic instruction. The school system is currently geared toward preparing students for college, but not all of them pursue a higher education. Some students need vocational training to prepare them to enter the workforce after high school. Offering vocational training will maintain their interest in school and in academics, she says.

* * *

Lucy Jones, Elementary School Teacher, New York

As a first grade teacher in a New York suburb, Lucy Jones often finds herself dealing with situations that fall outside the realm of academics. One afternoon after lunch, Ms. Jones' students filed into the classroom and sat on the rug for a read-aloud. Ms. Jones noticed that one of her students went directly to the bathroom. After a few minutes, the student opened the bathroom door, stood in the doorway with his pants around his ankles and shirt pulled up to his chin, and shouted, "I have diarrhea!"

Ms. Jones sent the other students to their seats to work while she attended to the child in the bathroom. When she walked into the bathroom, the child informed her that he didn't know how to clean himself. She gave him some toilet tissue, told him to clean his bottom, and left the bathroom. Shortly after, he called her again, claiming that the toilet tissue hurt. She looked in the toilet and saw that he had tried to use the toilet tissue, but she figured he must use moist wipes at home. She gave him a few wipes and told him they must be deposited in the garbage, not in the toilet.

Ms. Jones went back to her class, but soon the boy called her back into the bathroom because he needed more wipes. When she returned to the bathroom, she noticed the toilet tissue was no longer in the toilet. It was now in the garbage. The boy had misunderstood her warning about discarding the moist wipes in the garbage and not in the toilet. He thought her instructions applied to the toilet tissue as well. He had reached into the dirty toilet water, pulled out the toilet tissue, and placed it in the garbage. Now his arm was wet and dirty up to his elbow.

Astonished by the scene, she asked the student who cleans him at home, and he replied that his mother does. She estimates she spent about 30 minutes tending to the student while the rest of the class missed out on valuable instruction time. She questions why the student was not taught how to use the bathroom independently before being sent to school.

"Then the parents ask, 'Why are you not doing more math in the classroom?'" she says. "What you really want to say is 'because I'm spending 30 minutes wiping your kid's butt.'"

* * *

Disrespect

Nancy Davis, who has been teaching in New York City for 25 years, says student behavior has deteriorated in recent years because of the lack of discipline and because students who require special services are not receiving them. Students often yell and curse at their teachers. In the past, there was a line that the students knew they could not cross. "The line is now in China," she says.

Teachers in suburbia have also noted an increase in disrespectful attitudes and inappropriate remarks among their students. Some contend that the pervasiveness of new technology has spawned a teen-centric culture in which adolescents lack the ability to interact properly with adults. The proliferation of e-mail, instant messaging, cell phones, text messaging and social networking websites has created a close-knit teen community with its own language and knowledge base, further alienating parents and teachers as outsiders. The electronic world affords immediate access to friends and schoolmates around the clock, eliminating the need to call a friend's home telephone and politely address his or her parents.

Teachers in Ms. Davis' school feel hamstrung by weak policies regarding discipline. They are limited in their response to misconduct because out-of-school suspension has been eliminated as a disciplinary measure, and the in-school suspension room is often too full because the school accepts suspended students from other schools. Thus students have no deterrent to improper behavior.

Large class sizes exacerbate the problem. Ms. Davis, who teaches eighth grade English and social studies, has 32 to 33 students in her class. Her largest class size was 39 one year. The large class size means a larger percentage of students, in general, have behavior problems that persist for years.

Studies show that smaller class sizes not only lead to stronger academic achievement, but also reduce behavior problems. *Reducing Class Size: What Do We Know?* a study released by the U.S. Department of Education in 1998, found that smaller classes in the early grades improve student achievement and classroom discipline. A study released in 2003 by the American Educational Research Association reported that smaller classes are more effective due in large part to changes in student and teacher behavior. Students receive more individual attention from the teacher, which leads to increased participation in learning activities. As attention to learning increases, disruptive behavior declines, the study noted.

Rampant behavior problems and weak discipline policies in Ms. Davis' school have caused many teachers—newcomers and seasoned veterans—to quit. "Anybody who can get out is getting out," she says. Although the city is offering appealing compensation to attract good teachers, for many it's not worth it. "Mine is not such a horror story because I am a tough teacher," she says. But some of the newer teachers are having difficulty controlling their classrooms, and they refrain from involving the administration because they don't want to give the impression that they can't handle their jobs. When a classroom is out of control, "How much can the children be learning?" Ms. Davis says, adding that she has lost her passion for teaching.

* * *

Sarah Brown, Middle School Teacher, New York

Sarah Brown grew up around teachers. Her father was a teacher in New York City, and he often invited colleagues to their home. He was friendly with the administrators in the district where she attended elementary, middle and high school. When Ms. Brown was in middle school and high school, she enjoyed spending her free periods with her teachers. But she didn't plan to pursue a career as a teacher. She enjoyed mathematics, so she majored in finance in college. She held an internship at an investment banking firm during the summer before her junior year and decided it did not suit her. She switched her major to marketing, which didn't appeal to her either. Mulling over her career options, she considered how much she liked children. She had worked as a babysitter and camp counselor since she was 12 years old. Her senior year in college, she decided to take an internship position at a local elementary school to determine if she enjoyed teaching. The second semester of her senior year, she enrolled in the courses she needed to become a certified teacher and after graduation headed to graduate school to pursue a master's in education.

The relationships Ms. Brown formed with her middle school and high school teachers helped her land a position teaching sixth grade immediately after graduation. The school district, located in an affluent suburb of New York City, had a superb academic reputation and offered an attractive salary and benefits package to teachers. The competition for a teaching position in this highly esteemed school district was intense, and she felt fortunate to receive a job offer so early in her career.

She was surprised that some of the students had attitudes that differed drastically from the attitudes of her classmates when she attended the school. Several years after she was hired, she was teaching a lecture on listening skills in her sixth grade study skills class. She was constantly interrupted by a student who was uttering loud and discourteous remarks. At one point he referred to another student as "a fat lard." When she reached the part of her discussion about blocking out distractions and focusing on the teacher's lesson, she cited the student's outbursts as an example of such a distraction. Displeased, the student responded by stating, "If you didn't have tenure, I'd have you fired in two seconds." When she asked how he expected to execute his threat, he replied, "I would lie and say that you molested me or something."

Ms. Brown contends that the students at her school are too comfortable with their teachers and do not view them as authority figures. The students lack the ability to discern between appropriate and inappropriate remarks when interacting with teachers. On a field trip to a local theater, one of her male students asked her where they could find a private place to sit so they could have a date. Later in the year, when the same student received an 84% on his progress report, he said to her, "Yeah, this isn't going to work for me. You're going to need to raise this."

A colleague of Ms. Brown's, Peggy Scott, an eighth grade French teacher, says she has also encountered condescending attitudes among the students in her class. She had one of her classes for three straight years, and they had become too comfortable in her classroom. They were talkative, disruptive, and failed to pay attention. After three years of threatening them, she finally decided to rearrange their seats. She mapped out the new seating arrangement on the interactive white board. "They were groaning and grumbling," she says. "But I had tried everything else." When the room finally quieted down, Ms. Scott heard one of the girls utter, "Do I need to remind you my mother is on the board of education?"

She was taken aback, and she wasn't sure how to interpret the student's remark. "When she said it, I wasn't sure what she meant. 'If you don't keep me happy, I will complain to my mom?'"

Ms. Scott responded, "Are you threatening me?" The girl replied, "No, I'm just reminding you." During the exchange, the room was silent and tense as the other students' eyes darted from Ms. Scott to their classmate. "It was like watching a tennis match," Ms. Scott says.

She says some of her colleagues told her that the student's mother often mentions her position on the school board as well. But most of the parents are supportive. One parent, who was volunteering at the school shortly after the seating chart incident, stopped in to talk to Ms. Scott. The parent said her daughter had complained about the new seating arrangement, but that she supported Ms. Scott's decision. "Just tell her she has to sit there," the mother said.

Another sixth grade teacher at the same school, Rachel Bell, has been struggling with her weight for years and is sensitive about the issue. One of her students asked her "Were you at the Food Emporium yesterday?" She replied that she wasn't. The student said, "I thought I saw you at the all-you-can-eat buffet," and chuckled with his friends. Ms. Bell felt demoralized and humiliated.

A sixth grade girl in one of Judy White's classes asked her to step into the hallway because she had something to tell her privately. Ms. White went with the student into the hallway. The girl proceeded to inform her, "You really shouldn't wear white because your nipples are showing."

Students in Ms. Brown's school are not only disrespectful to their teachers, but they also demonstrate a lack of regard for school property. A student defecated in a bathroom sink on one occasion and on the bathroom floor on another. The fecal matter was discovered with a pencil sticking out of it. The perpetrator was never discovered. On another occasion, a male student urinated on the gym lockers.

In addition to making inappropriate comments directly to her, many of Ms. Brown's students disrespect her authority by failing to exhibit proper behavior during her class. They disrupt her lessons by blatantly injecting comments and carrying on conversations, making no attempt to prevent her from hearing them. She was in the middle of presenting a lesson to her sixth grade math strategies class when one of the students reached into his pocket, pulled out a condom and shouted, "This is my brother's jacket! He has a condom in it! He doesn't even have a girlfriend." Another student in the class replied, "At least you know he doesn't have a boyfriend." The first student said, "He would need a condom then, too!" Attempting to end the dialogue and regain control of the class, she stated, "That's something you can discuss in health class," and returned to her lesson.

When she noticed a student chewing gum during class, Ms. Brown directed the student to discard the gum. The girl walked over to the wastebasket, tossed out the gum, and returned to her desk. A few minutes later, Ms. Brown noticed the same student chewing gum. "Did you not spit out the gum or is that a new piece?" Ms. Brown inquired. "It's a new piece," the student replied. "Did you think I just didn't like the original piece of gum?" Ms. Brown said sarcastically. "Please spit out that piece of gum and do not chew any piece of gum during class."

On another occasion, Ms. Brown was helping one student when another student sitting at the desk behind her began shouting, "Child abuse, child abuse!" She turned around to find the student had wrapped heavy-duty tape around his chest and the back of the chair, effectively securing himself to the chair and rendering himself immobile.

Aggravating incidences such as these cause stress and frustration to well up inside her during class. At the end of the day, she distances herself from her job by leaving her work at school. This helps her handle the stress and remain enthusiastic about her job. When she deals with students who are constantly disrespectful and disruptive, she reminds herself that she has to deal with them for only one year and then they move on (although she acknowledges that she will probably have problems with some of her new students the following year). In addition, she focuses on the positive aspects of her job, which outweigh the negative. While some of her students have attitude problems, most of them don't. One year was particularly hard because most of the students in the sixth grade that year were difficult. But the following year brought a new group of students who behaved better on the whole. Most importantly, when a lesson registers with her students and they get it, it's a rewarding and fulfilling experience.

* * *

Lynn Randolph, High School Teacher, Ohio

Lynn Randolph pursued a degree in journalism with a minor in English in college. Her junior year she decided she would prefer to write for magazines rather than newspapers, so she decided to major in English and minor in journalism. She was a member of the honors college at her university. The dean sent an e-mail message to the honors college students to ask if anyone would be interested in tutoring local high school students. She signed up to tutor a couple of days a week. "I loved it. I hated going back to my journalism courses. I would rather be at the high school all the time working with the kids," she says.

When she graduated, she decided she wanted to be a teacher, and enrolled in a graduate school to receive a master's degree in education.

Her first teaching job was at a high school in Ohio near where she grew up. She taught English and journalism for grades nine through 12. She taught five courses—journalism, a journalism class that integrated the yearbook, junior English, and two senior English courses tied to vocational programs (one for students studying to be firefighters or emergency medical technicians and another for students studying to be Web designers).

She also served as the assistant advisor for the student newspaper and advisor for the extracurricular yearbook activities. The newspaper was published every other week. Prior to the publication of each edition, she spent two to three nights that week at school until 9 or 10 p.m.

As a young teacher, Ms. Randolph found that working with high school students, particularly seniors, was challenging. On her first day, she was standing outside the classroom, professionally dressed in a pantsuit, when the students began to walk in. A few of them asked her if she knew who their teacher was going to be. When she told them it was her, they expressed disbelief, shouting, "No way!" and running down the hall to tell their friends.

She decided she should give them the impression that she was going to be tough and firm so they would respect her authority. She did not want them to think they could take advantage of her youth and inexperience. And she had been given the advice that is often given to new teachers: "Don't smile until Christmas." (Some say, "Don't smile until Christmas and you'll smile until June.") "I didn't want them to walk all over me," Ms. Randolph says. "Any sign of weakness, they'll smell it."

Later in the lunchroom, a colleague told Ms. Randolph that she overheard a boy talking about her. She asked what he said. The colleague said, "He said you're a real bitch."

"I wanted to cry," she says. "I was so devastated. I wanted them to respect me, but still like me."

Her attempt to command respect backfired, as did her efforts to relate to the students. When she introduced herself to the students on her first day, she told them she was familiar with their community because she attended a nearby high school. But the school she attended had a reputation for being located in a "snobby, affluent area," which turned the students off. "You look like you went there," one girl scoffed. It reminded her of the time when she was a student teacher at another nearby high school; the students there booed her when she told them where she attended high school.

In the middle of a presentation to the class, one of the boys gestured with his middle finger to a student in the classroom who made a face at him. The class turned and looked at Ms. Randolph, who was sitting in the back of the room, to see how she would react. She told the student to see her after class. When he approached her after class, he arrogantly and nonchalantly asked her what she wanted to see him about, pretending not to acknowledge his offensive behavior during his presentation. He even asked her if she wanted to see him because he made a derogatory remark about the high school she attended earlier in the class. She told him she would have to report him because of the crude gesture he made during his presentation. He apathetically shrugged and said, "Oh."

"I was in shock," she says. "He wouldn't have done that to an older teacher."

The lack of respect she received from other teachers on the staff did not help the students to view her as an authority figure. One of the teachers yelled at her for using the copy machine in the copy room, bellowing, "You're not supposed to be in here. Students are not allowed in here." She was wearing her ID badge around her neck at the time.

When the hallway was blocked off to student traffic because a test was being administered, the teacher monitoring the hallway refused to let her pass, mistaking her for a student. All of the students who were traveling through the hallway on their way to class witnessed the altercation and laughed.

The newspaper advisor she worked with treated her with a condescending attitude. He was training her to take over for him as advisor because he planned to leave the school at the end of the year. He would enter her classroom, slap her on the back and say, "Hey, kiddo." He put so much pressure on her to be dedicated to the job that she felt his behavior approached harassment. He would tell her that he was concerned she would get married and her husband wouldn't understand that she needed to be at the newspaper all the time. When she mentioned that she planned to have children one day, he warned her that she better not.

Ms. Randolph felt she took on too much her first year, with five different classes to prepare for, nearly 150 students to grade, and two extracurricular activities. She approached the administration at the end of the year and requested a change. She said she needed to focus on English and the yearbook, or focus on journalism and the newspaper, but she could not handle both. Because the school planned to hire a new teacher to replace the journalism teacher who worked with her on the newspaper, she suggested splitting journalism and English—and their related activities—between her and the new teacher. The principal refused her request.

She did not want to take on another year with an overwhelming workload. She and a friend had been talking about moving to Florida. She decided to go, and she resigned her position at the high school.

Before she left, the assistant principal apologized to her. He said he regretted that she received such a heavy workload her first year and he didn't blame her for leaving. He said the principal's expectations were unrealistic, and the administration should have accommodated her request so that she would stay. After she left, she heard from her sister-in-law, who taught at the school, that the administration ultimately took her suggestion and split the journalism and English departments.

At the beginning of the year, she had hoped the students would immediately support her and view her as a new teacher who brought enthusiasm and fresh ideas to the classroom. But they just viewed her as a young, inexperienced teacher who was not worthy of their respect. She worked hard to earn their respect throughout the year, and she eventually accomplished this feat. "I was surprised that it wasn't easier to win them over," she says.

When the students found out she was leaving, they gave her cards, letters and gifts. She received a bucket with assorted items suitable for the beach, such as flip-flops and sunglasses, because she planned to move to Florida. It was left on the doorstep at her home. When the newspaper advisor found out she was leaving, he refused to talk to her for the remainder of the school year.

Ms. Randolph taught eighth grade language arts in Florida. The librarian was about to retire and "she didn't want to deal with anybody," so she locked the library door all day. "I never took my kids to the library."

Her negative experience with the school library in Florida prompted her to consider becoming a media specialist. She found it frustrating that her workload prevented her from keeping up with young adult literature and recommending books to her students. She decided to pursue a master's degree in library science after teaching in Florida for only a year. She then took a job as a media specialist at a school in Ohio. She spent two years in the position before getting married and moving to Georgia to be with her husband, who is in the U.S. military.

She enjoys her current job as a media specialist in a Georgia school system because it affords her the opportunity to work with all of the students in the school, to promote reading for pleasure rather than for homework, and to teach classes about library research.

* * *

Nicole Evans, Elementary School Teacher, Connecticut

When Nicole Evans was a child, she often pretended to be a teacher. "My parents bought me a giant chalkboard that was on wheels and it flipped over. There was a blackboard on one side and a green board on the other," she says. "My mom brought home carbon copy paper from work, and I would make worksheets and have the entire neighborhood over to play."

During college, she worked with homeless and neglected children. "It was then that I realized I needed to be a teacher and be the one that gave these children the proper foundation in order to be successful," she says. "I have always felt that my professional goal was to inspire children."

She earned a bachelor of arts in psychology and planned to be a school psychologist. Because such jobs were scarce, she pursued her master's degree in elementary education and special education as a fallback. She taught preschool in Massachusetts and New York while pursuing her master's and continued to teach preschool for the next five years. Following her stint as a preschool teacher, she taught fifth grade and kindergarten in New York City. She is currently working in Connecticut, where she has been teaching third and fourth grade (looped classes) for the past six years. (When a teacher retains the same class for two successive years, this is known as "looping".)

She says she is surprised by the lack of respect the students have for adults. She has worked with children from a variety of backgrounds—homeless, neglected, inner-city, poor, middle class and upper class—for the past 13 years. Regardless of their backgrounds, many children do not demonstrate respect for adults, she says.

"It has become a serious problem in school with children talking back and not taking what you say seriously," she says. Children come to school with "a great deal of baggage" and teachers are expected to wear a variety of hats to deal with them—social worker, psychologist, nurse, disciplinarian, parent. "Actual teaching takes a back seat to all the emotional and behavioral issues that occur on a daily basis," she says.

* * *

Marcia James, High School Teacher, New York

When Marcia James decided to become a teacher 10 years ago, she visited the schools in her neighborhood in New York City with her art portfolio, looking for a position as an art teacher. She doesn't drive and wanted to work close to home. At first she worked as a substitute teacher in various schools. She substituted for classroom teachers and consistently tried to inject art into the lessons the teachers prepared for her. For example, she would read a story and create an art project based on the story. One of the elementary schools where she worked offered her a full-time position. "They liked me. They said I actually did something. Most subs are just babysitters," she says.

At about the same time, the elementary school was combined with the middle school, making it a K-8 school. Also at that time, the school applied for and received a grant from a private individual to fund its art program. One of the middle school teachers who had an interest in art and was teaching art out of her classroom was placed in charge of allocating the grant money and purchasing art supplies. Ms. James was offered the art teacher position in the middle school. Before the new art supplies were ordered and received, she had only a box of crayons to work with. She doesn't remember exactly how she taught the class with no supplies, but she recalls trying to ascertain what the students liked to do and attempting to appeal to their interests.

Because the school was overcrowded, some of the classes were set up in annexes—two separate buildings located in the neighborhood. She didn't have an art room and had to carry her art supplies from classroom to classroom and from building to building. This concept is known as "art from a cart." "It is the stupidest thing that has ever been created on this planet," she says. The other specialists, such as the reading teachers, also had to travel from classroom to classroom, but she had to carry all of her supplies with her.

The most difficult aspect of the situation was the lack of respect the students showed her, she says. A teacher coming into another teacher's classroom is treated like a substitute by the students, not as a regular teacher. Some of the teachers demanded their students respect the teachers who came into the classroom, but others did not. Some stayed for the art lesson, but most took advantage of the break to prepare lessons, eat lunch or use the bathroom. Some of the teachers were annoyed when Ms. James was late because it cut into their break time. "To get a bathroom break or go to lunch is a big deal," she says.

One of the teachers who stayed in the classroom reprimanded her students one day for misbehaving during Ms. James' art lesson. "She let the kids have it, but she did it in a nice way. She explained to them that I was trying to do this wonderful thing with them," Ms. James says. "Here I am feeling like a poor slob, and she's making me sound like a princess. She made me feel better about myself."

She acknowledges that many occupations are stressful, but the issues teachers face are unique because they involve children. "A first grader may stand up on a table and start acting like Tarzan," she says, noting this is not something an employee in the corporate world is likely to face.

Disrespectful and inappropriate behavior can be infuriating, she says. "Sometimes you want to take their head and put it through a wall, but you can't touch them." Even when teachers restrain their verbal responses, they can get into trouble. When Ms. James was supervising an exam, one of the girls in the class stood up and moved her seat. Ms. James told the student she was not permitted to get up and walk around during a test. Later, Ms. James was summoned to the principal's office. The principal said the girl claimed Ms. James called her a bitch. "I looked her in the face and I said 'I swear to you, I didn't say that.'" It was then that she realized how precarious her job was. "You can lose your job over a lie," she says.

Her job also depended on her ability to adhere to the school district's policies, which were communicated in numerous memos, because board of education members often visited the school to observe. For example, she was not permitted to place student artwork on bulletin boards unless it was accompanied by written work to demonstrate the school was focusing on literacy. To accomplish this task, she had to work with the classroom teachers, many of whom were already overextended and had limited time to contribute to her art curriculum. Eventually, she worked with the students and teachers to create an entire school art show. The students' artwork was displayed at a local college. Many of the teachers helped put up and take down the artwork, and they did not receive additional compensation for their time.

Despite her struggles, she remained at her job because she felt trapped. She had tried other jobs before teaching. She went to art school, worked as a freelancer in the art world and as a photographer. When she was in her 30s, she felt she needed steady, full-time work. Her friend suggested she go back to school to become a teacher because she liked kids. "I had other jobs and they didn't last," she says. She decided to take her friend's advice and go back to college to become an art teacher. Now, she's reluctant to change jobs again, particularly after investing the time and money into obtaining her teaching credentials. "I figured, this is it. I have to make a living," she says. "I can't walk away from this."

After about five or six years, a new principal came into the school and decided she didn't have the money in the budget for Ms. James' position. She was "excessed," which basically means she was let go because her position was unnecessary. "The board of education comes up with these words and you have no idea what the hell they're talking about. They have their own private language," she says.

She found a job teaching art at an alternative high school. Some of her students were as old as 21, some had served time in prison, some were parents. "This was their last chance to get their degrees," she says. "I didn't really know what I was getting into, but I felt good about the principal at the time." Her commute was about an hour on the bus and subways.

The school building was "ancient," she says. "The bathrooms were from the year of the flood." Teachers didn't have separate bathroom facilities and were forced to share with the students. "Do you know how demeaning that is?" She says she tried to use the bathroom facilities when students weren't in there, but that was not always possible.

She says she does not have an assertive personality, but she had to become harder and tougher to deal with her students. When one of her students cursed at her, "I walked up to him and said, 'What did you say to me?'" He cursed again, and she said, "Excuse me, I'm a teacher." His reply was, "So what." She didn't feel hurt because she knew there was most likely something on the student's mind that caused him to lash out at her.

"A lot of these kids are angry and they need a lot of help," she says. She asked an administrator who was walking by to come into the classroom. He brought the student into the hall and spoke with him. When the student returned, he mumbled an apology to her.

She feels conflicting emotions toward her students—she feels compassion for them because of the difficult experiences they've faced in their lives, but she also feels upset with them for their behavior toward her. "You have to feel bad for them on one hand, but on the other hand, I'm exhausted. When I come home, I just want to go to sleep."

She says her job involves so much more than academics, and she's not trained to handle it. "I'm not a therapist, I'm not a social worker," she says. "You have to be a magician to handle all these things," she says. "It's everything but teaching."

Ms. James says the reason teachers have summers off is they need the break from their lives as teachers. "We need time to become people again. It takes all of your energy out of you," she says. She recently bumped into a retired teacher she knew at a bookstore, and the woman looked like a different person because she had eliminated the stress of teaching from her life.

Ms. James is seeing a therapist to help her cope. "I need a way to handle this," she says, adding that she doesn't want to burden her friends and family with stories about her plight.

Although Ms. James, now in her 50s, still feels trapped in her job, she admits, "I don't think I'm going to survive much longer." She was recently "excessed" again and has to find another position. "I'm back where I started 10 years ago," she says. "I didn't think it was going to be like this."

But she is determined to stay with teaching until she receives her "longevity" pay increase after she reaches 10 years. "It's like combat pay. I deserve it and I need it," she says. "Sometimes I think I probably should have done something different with my life."

Chapter Three

Parents–
Allies or Adversaries

*"At some point, teachers and parents stopped working
together and started working against each other."*

Jane Miller, Middle School Teacher, Florida

Academics

Joseph Dunn, High School Teacher, New Jersey

When Joseph Dunn was in high school, he found himself
constantly assessing the teaching styles and approaches of his teachers.

He watched them carefully, taking mental notes about teaching. He evaluated the effectiveness of their techniques. Whether his interest in teaching grew out of this habit, or whether a propensity toward the profession was in his blood (his father was a teacher), he decided to pursue a career in the education field.

He was always interested in the subject of history. After college, he obtained a position as a history teacher for 10th, 11th and 12th graders at a private school. After three years, he was hired as a 10th grade history teacher at a public high school in New Jersey. He recently completed his first year.

Mr. Dunn says dealing with parents is the most frustrating aspect of his job. "Parents of this generation are overbearing," he says. They are also quick to blame the teacher if a child is unhappy or performing poorly. "If something happens in the classroom, and the kid says to the parents, 'This happened,' you'll get a call from the parents asking, 'What should we do about what you did to my child?' not 'What should we do about my child?'" He says this attitude contrasts sharply with the mindset of his own parents' generation. "When I was a student, my parents would be like, 'What's wrong with you?'" he says.

The mother of one of his students requested a conference because her daughter was not performing well in his Advanced Placement (college level) class. "She had to find a reason," he says. At the conference, the mother blamed her daughter's poor performance on the school's failure to provide her daughter with the summer reading assignment. The father, an attorney, was present through the speaker-phone and he was "irate," Mr. Dunn says.

The reading assignment was distributed at the end of the previous year, but the student claimed she never received it. The assignment was handed out before Mr. Dunn was hired, but every student was required to sign an agreement acknowledging that he or she received the assignment and would complete it over the summer. Mr. Dunn had the signed agreements and knew the student was lying to her parents, but he also knew it would inflame the confrontation if he accused their daughter of lying.

"You could hear him breathing heavy on the phone. The last thing you want to do is say, 'Your daughter is lying to you.' You have to be delicate about it," Mr. Dunn says. He and his department head, who was also present at the conference, circumvented this issue by reassuring the parents that their daughter's grades were where they should be at this point in the year and that it takes time for students to adjust to the class' higher level.

The parents continued to press the issue of the reading assignment. The department head slid the reading assignment across the table to the mother. "You could see behind the mother's eyes, something clicked—she probably did get it and she just didn't do it," Mr. Dunn says. At that point, he thought to himself, "You're just wasting my time." He had spent 20 minutes of his day—time he could have invested in grading papers or planning lessons—on a parent-teacher conference because the parents refused to acknowledge that their daughter did not do her homework.

Mr. Dunn believes some parents pressure their children and push them too hard. One of his students lacked the academic skills required for his regular class, and he felt she would have benefited more from a remedial class. But her parents insisted on placing her in his class. He found out that the girl's older brother was a highly successful student and was attending a prestigious university. He speculated that the parents had the same expectations for their daughter and could not accept that she was not as gifted academically. Aside from her academic limitations, she had learning disabilities and was entitled to certain accommodations. For instance, she received extra time on exams. In addition, he had to make up a special exam for her that offered three multiple-choice answers rather than his usual four.

The girl's parents told her to request more accommodations than she is legally entitled to. For example, she requested he give her quizzes that were multiple choice rather than short answer because she has difficulty with written work. He says he responded to her requests in the beginning of the year because he was a new teacher and she caught him off guard. "I was trying to do right by her. But then I realized I wasn't doing her any favors," he says, adding that he felt strongly that she should learn how to write.

The student continued to avoid writing essays in class after her parents and case manager at the school agreed she could verbally communicate her responses to open-ended questions on quizzes and exams.

But the homework assignments required writing. Because the student felt pressured to live up to her parents' expectations, she plagiarized a homework paper, Mr. Dunn says. "Her parents put her in that position."

He tried to be sympathetic to her situation. He told her he was aware she plagiarized but that she would not be punished. He admonished her not to do it again because he might not be so understanding the next time.

The student's parents seemed more concerned with her grades than with the knowledge and skills she attained in school. Her grades were artificially inflated due to the accommodations her parents worked out with her case manager. "Because of her accommodations, she'll get an A, but she's learned nothing and she has no skills," Mr. Dunn says.

The student's parents never contacted Mr. Dunn directly. They always discussed issues with her case manager at the school, and the case manager would communicate to Mr. Dunn the accommodations he would be expected to provide.

He found it difficult to comply with all of the student's accommodations and teach 23 other students in the class at the same time. It was helpful for him to talk to a colleague who had the same student and was dealing with similar issues. She empathized with his situation and offered advice.

Mr. Dunn questions the efficacy of artificially bolstering grades by implementing accommodations. "They are there to appease the parents," he says. But accommodations don't necessarily help the students because they won't have the benefit of accommodations in the real world, he says. He has students in his classes who are allowed to take a test over and over until they achieve a B. "It does not serve the kids. It's problematic," he says.

In his Advanced Placement class, he had a student who is allowed extra time on exams because he suffers from anxiety, which causes him to lose concentration. The student's anxiety stems from the pressure his mother puts on him, Mr. Dunn maintains. He says the student would not have anxiety issues if he were in a regular level class rather than an Advanced Placement class.

The student's mother brought him along to a parent-teacher conference. Mr. Dunn, a non-tenured teacher, says he was not assertive enough to ask her to leave her son outside the room during the conference. He was forced to discuss the student's performance in front of him, and sit there uncomfortably while the mother turned to her son and asked, "Do you understand what he's saying?" Mr. Dunn says the situation was humiliating for the student, and the mother should have discussed the conference with her son when they arrived home, not in front of his teacher. The mother insisted that her son must have a learning disability because he wasn't excelling in the Advanced Placement course. Mr. Dunn doesn't believe the student has a learning disability.

"He's an average student, and his mother can't accept it," he says. Mr. Dunn says his college-level history course is not for everyone, but some parents fail to acknowledge that their children are going to excel in some areas and not in others. They expect their children to excel at everything.

In addition to the widespread use of accommodations, Mr. Dunn says the school is too lenient on students in other ways. They are not penalized for arriving late to school. "The most basic thing you can teach a student is you have got to show up on time. If you can't teach them that, they are never going to hold down a job," he says, adding that children need structure and rules.

Mr. Dunn says teaching is like "death by 1,000 cuts." A lot of little things day after day can wear a teacher down. "You're dealing with 100 kids in a single day. You're in charge of them for 80 minutes." Not only do teachers have to teach their students, but they also have to deal with interpersonal issues, he says.

"You come home exhausted," he says. But there is always more work to do—more lessons to plan and more papers to grade. "You can literally work until you go to bed," he says. "We do need summers off because we need time to recharge our batteries."

* * *

Studies show that parental involvement in a child's education is a major factor in determining academic success, regardless of economic, ethnic or cultural background, according to the National Parent Teacher Association (PTA). Parental involvement also contributes to better school attendance, improved rates of homework completion, decreased violence and substance abuse, and higher graduation rates. To encourage parental involvement in the school community, local PTAs around the country organize events that bring families and school faculty together, and they create opportunities for parents to volunteer in the school and classroom.

On the National PTA's top 10 list of things teachers wish parents would do, "be involved" ranks number one (see sidebar). Also on the list is to "call teachers early if you think there's a problem," rather than wait for the teacher to reach out.

While parental participation is vital to a student's academic success, problems arise when the parent's involvement becomes excessive and the parent ceases to collaborate with the teacher in a constructive partnership. When a parent declines to consider the teacher's input, fails to value the teacher's expertise, and makes unrealistic demands, the situation can become frustrating and stressful for the teacher.

A lack of parental involvement is a challenging issue as well. Barbara Martin, a former guidance counselor at an inner-city school district in Nevada, was rarely able to reach parents with a concern about a student, and her messages were not returned. The school's contact information was often out of date because families moved around so much. Many of the children took care of themselves after school, or were cared for by an older sibling, because their parents had to work at two jobs. They were unavailable to encourage their children to do their homework or to help them with it. Some of the children had serious issues, such as depression, but were not receiving the medical attention they needed because of a lack of health insurance. Sometimes a child she was working with would just disappear. She spent one year at an elementary school in the district and two at a middle school before resigning. "I only lasted three years before burnout," she says.

Top 10 Things Teachers Wish Parents Would Do

◆ **Be involved.**

Parent involvement helps students learn, improves schools, and allows teachers to work with you to help your children succeed.

◆ **Provide resources at home for learning.**

Utilize your local library, stock your home with books and magazines, and read with your children every day.

◆ **Set a good example.**

Show your children that you believe reading is enjoyable and useful.

◆ **Encourage students to do their best in school.**

Communicate to your children that you believe education is important and you want them to do their best.

◆ **Value education and seek a balance between schoolwork and outside activities.**

Emphasize your children's progress in developing the knowledge and skills they need to succeed in school and life.

◆ **Recognize factors that take a toll on students' classroom performance.**

Help your children maintain a balance between school responsibilities and outside commitments.

◆ **Support school rules and goals.**

Avoid undermining school rules, discipline or goals.

◆ **Use pressure positively.**

Encourage children to do their best, but avoid pressuring them by setting goals too high or scheduling too many activities.

◆ **Call teachers early if you think there's a problem.**
Address a problem while there is still time to solve it, rather than waiting for the teacher's call.

◆ **Accept your responsibility as parents.**
Teach your children self-discipline and respect for others rather than relying on schools to teach these basic behaviors.

Source: National PTA (www.pta.org).

Laura Taylor, a former elementary school teacher in an urban New York community, says parent-teacher conference day was largely a day off for her. "If five parents showed up, it was a lot," she says.

Meanwhile, parents who are overly involved in their child's education are often referred to as "helicopter parents." Wikipedia defines helicopter parent as follows:

"A helicopter parent is a term for a person who pays extremely close attention to his or her child or children, particularly at educational institutions. They rush to prevent any harm or failure from befalling them or letting them learn from their own mistakes, sometimes even contrary to the children's wishes. They are so named because, like a helicopter, they hover closely overhead, rarely out of reach whether their children need them or not. An extension of the term, "Black Hawks," has been coined for those who cross the line from a mere excess of zeal to unethical behavior such as writing their children's college admissions essays. (The reference is to the military helicopter of the same name.)"

Fueling the aggressive behavior of helicopter parents is the intense competition for college admissions. According to an article in the April 4, 2007, edition of *The New York Times*, the spring of 2007 was the most selective in modern memory at America's top schools, as college admissions offices were inundated with more applications than in any previous year on record. Harvard turned down more than 1,000 candidates with perfect 800 scores on the SAT math exam; Yale rejected several applicants with perfect 2,400 scores on the three-part SAT; and Princeton rejected thousands of applicants with 4.0 grade point averages, the article stated. The bevy of applications to top schools, which resulted in low acceptance rates, stems from three factors, according to college admissions officers interviewed for the *Times* article: Children of baby boomers are graduating from high school in large numbers, more high school students are enrolling in college immediately after graduation, and the average candidate applies to more colleges than in the past due in part to the convenience of the Common Application, which can be submitted via the Internet. Applications to top colleges and universities hit record levels again by early 2008, according to an article in the Jan. 17, 2008, edition of *The New York Times*.

Most teachers welcome parental involvement and understand that only by working with parents can they achieve success. But it is important for parents to approach teachers as partners and strive to cultivate productive relationships. To foster healthy and effective relationships between parents and schools, the National PTA developed "National Standards for Family-School Partnerships" (see sidebar). The National PTA offers local PTAs a plethora of ideas for implementing the standards put forth.

PTA's National Standards for Family-School Partnerships

Standard 1: Welcoming All Families into the School Community: Families are active participants in the life of the school, and feel welcomed, valued, and connected to each other, to school staff, and to what students are learning and doing in class.

Standard 2: Communicating Effectively: Families and school staff engage in regular, meaningful communication about student learning.

Standard 3: Supporting Student Success: Families and school staff continuously collaborate to support students' learning and healthy development both at home and school, and have regular opportunities to strengthen their knowledge and skills to do so effectively.

Standard 4: Speaking Up for Every Child: Families are empowered to be advocates for their own and other children to ensure that students are treated fairly and have access to learning opportunities that will support their success.

Standard 5: Sharing Power: Families and school staff are equal partners in decisions that affect children and families, and together inform, influence, and create policies, practices, and programs.

Standard 6: Collaborating with Community: Families and school staff collaborate with community members to connect students, families, and staff to expanded learning opportunities, community services, and civic participation.

Source: National PTA (www.pta.org).

* * *

Erica Stevens, High School Teacher, Massachusetts

Erica Stevens decided in fourth grade that she wanted to be a teacher. She thought all of the teachers played on the climbing equipment after school, and believed if she became a teacher she would have the same privilege. While her motivation eventually changed, she remained focused on her career goal. After she graduated from college, she joined Teach For America. (The Teach For America program recruits top college graduates to commit to teaching in low-income communities for two years.) She was placed in a high school in Los Angeles as an English teacher. After six years teaching in Los Angeles, she moved to Massachusetts (Ms. Stevens' experience in California is covered in Chapter 5).

Ms. Stevens spent a year as a reading specialist at an elementary school in Massachusetts, teaching a first grade class and a fourth and fifth combination class. She then took a job in an affluent area teaching high school English. The position represented a departure from her inner-city experience in Los Angeles, which she relished, despite the difficult issues she dealt with. She says the fulfillment she felt when she got through to her students kept her going. "I felt like what I was doing was important," she says. She encouraged her students to set their sights on college, helped them prepare for the SATs, and encouraged them to set goals for their lives.

In her new school in Massachusetts, where she has taught for four years, she doesn't have to push her students to set lofty goals because their parents do. She had a student in her ninth grade English class who was transferred from another class because of problems between the girl's parents and the other teacher. The student refused to do her homework, and her parents blamed it on a learning disability. They retained a psychologist to support their assertion and a lawyer to force the school to accommodate what they perceived to be their daughter's special needs. "Educational psychologists will always find something. They will take a natural weakness and say it's a deficit and slap a label on it," she asserts.

The student was a talented creative writer and always completed assignments involving creative writing. But she avoided analytical essays. The rest of the class was progressing, and she was falling behind because of her lack of attention to the homework.

The girl's parents convinced her she was disabled. Ms. Stevens overheard her discussing her disability with the other students.

When the student did not turn in her homework, her parents claimed she could not be penalized because of her disability. They continuously pressured Ms. Stevens to give their daughter a pass on the homework. Their behavior bordered on harassment, she says.

Still, the student continued to excel at creative writing. She was a gifted poet and served as the emcee for the school's evening poetry reading. Ms. Stevens was proud of her performance, and the event was a success. After the reading, when all of the parents were enjoying refreshments, the girl's parents cornered Ms. Stevens and pressured her to ignore their daughter's latest transgression when assigning her a grade. They e-mailed her the next morning to follow up. The principal asked the parents to back off, but they continued to press the issue.

Ms. Stevens went to the bookstore one evening. She parked two blocks away. During her walk to the bookstore, she noticed the girl's father in a restaurant window she passed. She saw him bolt for the door. She started running down the sidewalk. He chased her, calling her name. He caught up with her at the bookstore and again began badgering her about the homework issue.

Ms. Stevens was able to manage the situation because the student liked her. Ms. Stevens attempted to come up with solutions to the problem and ran them by the student to get her buy-in before talking to her parents.

"Unfortunately, by the end of the year she was the worst in the room when it came to analytical writing," Ms. Stevens says. The girl ended up with a C on her report card, which Ms. Stevens calls a compromise. But her parents insisted on placing her in honors English in 10th grade.

"We've just completely lost sight of what school is supposed to be for," Ms. Stevens says. "It's become a quest to look good for college.

It's all about looking good, getting the right grades, and participating in the right activities, not about actually learning."

* * *

Behavior

The partnership between parents and teachers transcends academics; it plays a major role in eliciting proper and respectful behavior from students when they are in school. Among the top 10 things teachers wish parents would do is "accept your responsibility as parents" and "support school rules and goals," according to the National PTA (see sidebar). Teachers rely on parents to instruct their children to respect their teachers and behave properly in school. When parents don't fulfill this obligation, it places an additional burden on teachers. When Deborah Clark, a fourth grade teacher, told a mother during a conference that her daughter's disrespectful attitude was out of control, the mother refused to discipline her daughter because she did not want to evoke anger from the child. She advised Ms. Clark that she would have to handle the problem herself. A more troublesome situation for teachers arises when a parent refuses to support disciplinary action or offers up excuses for the child's behavior.

* * *

Michael Duncan, Elementary School Teacher, California

Michael Duncan held a variety of jobs before becoming a teacher.

He was a heavy truck mechanic, a massage therapist and a chef. But he always wanted to be a teacher and finally decided to go back to school to obtain his credentials.

Mr. Duncan has been teaching third grade at a California elementary school for three years and loves his job. "I am rewarded every day," he says. "The majority of the students and their families are great. I have become a better teacher, and I have found ways to meet the needs of demanding parents." While he has become more adept at addressing parents' demands, he continues to wrestle with the problems he has dealing with parents who are unsupportive.

In his first year, a student was transferred into his class because the student's mother did not like the previous two teachers he was assigned to that year. The student's mother would leave 20-minute phone messages on his voice mail every day; listening to them would consume his entire free period. In addition to the barrage of phone messages, she frequently requested conferences or appeared without an appointment. He would walk into his classroom to find her sitting there waiting for him.

The woman's concern for her son was justified, Mr. Duncan says. The boy was unable to control his behavior and often disrupted the class by making strange noises. He lacked social skills and had difficulty getting along with the other students. Mr. Duncan assured the woman that he was diligently working with her son to resolve these problems. Yet she continued to demand his time and attention. Finally, Mr. Duncan expressed his concerns about the woman's behavior at a conference in which she and the principal were both present. The woman cried and apologized.

Mr. Duncan says teachers are well-trained to handle the academic aspects of their jobs, but they are often unprepared to deal with children who have behavioral, emotional or social problems. They are also unprepared to deal with overzealous parents.

To foster communication with parents, Mr. Duncan sends home planners on a regular basis. The planners contain assignments for the students and notes to the parents. A student in his class forged his father's signature on the planner. The student was falling behind in his work because he was not paying attention in class and lacked focus. Mr. Duncan contacted the parents, and they assured him they would address the problem with their son. They all agreed to make a fresh start after the school break. Following the break, the student was caught stealing two slices of pizza from the school cafeteria, an offense he denied. The father visited the school, expecting to meet with the principal. The principal was dealing with another matter, and the assistant principal met with the father. Because the principal didn't acknowledge the situation—and the student vehemently denied the accusation—the father concluded that Mr. Duncan and his colleagues were mistaken. Subsequently, Mr. Duncan sensed the father's mistrust in his tone on the telephone and in his refusal to sign the planners.

The student's social and behavioral issues affected his academic performance. Due to the lack of support Mr. Duncan received from the student's parents, the situation deteriorated. The boy was frequently involved in altercations with other students—stealing from them, calling them names and physically attacking them. His homework reflected a lack of parental involvement. Mr. Duncan was concerned not only for the student but also for himself because if the student was unable to handle fourth grade, Mr. Duncan knew he would be blamed.

Dealing with uncooperative parents creates severe stress for Mr. Duncan. "I still do not deal with this situation very well. I lose a lot of sleep trying to figure out how to help students who come from families where education is not a priority," he says. "It is very hard to see a child's potential and not be able to motive them." He has endured health issues related to the stress. "I am working on it though," he says.

* * *

Jane Miller, Middle School Teacher, Florida

Jane Miller majored in education, but the courses she took at her two-year college did not transfer to her four-year college in California. She decided to pursue a degree in public administration and planned to go into public policy or public health care. She ended up in retail management for a few years, but was displeased with her career choice. When she moved to Florida, she resumed her original plan and became a teacher.

She taught fourth grade at a private school for one year and taught for one school semester and the summer semester at an alternative high school for expelled students. She currently teaches grades six through eight at a public middle school in an affluent community. She has been a teacher in the school district for the past 11 years.

Last year she had a student in her class who often made offensive comments. After he proclaimed, "All women are good for is rape," Ms. Miller notified his parents. His father failed to acknowledge the seriousness of the boy's remark, claiming that his son didn't really mean what he said and that he was not given a chance to explain himself. The same student also told a classmate who was of Middle Eastern descent to "Go blow something up because that's what you guys do." Again, she called the student's parents, who declined to take any action.

On another occasion last year, Ms. Miller told a girl who was late for a third time that she had to serve detention due to school policy. The student protested, claiming she was being treated unfairly and that she refused to serve the detention. She contacted her mother on her cell phone and vehemently complained about Ms. Miller's actions, portraying them inaccurately. The student succeeded in riling up her mother, who yelled at Ms. Miller and accused her of treating her daughter unfairly. The mother eventually apologized after Ms. Miller had a chance to explain the situation at a conference.

Ms. Miller says some of her students are not motivated to behave properly because they do not receive any discipline at home. The students exude a "sense of entitlement," she says, adding that they have "a poor work ethic and a skewed value system. Education is not viewed as important."

Some parents do attempt to convey to their children the importance of working hard and achieving success in school, but the message is lost in a sea of iPods, cell phones and designer clothing, she says. Other parents fail to support her attempts to encourage students to conduct themselves properly in school and to demonstrate respect for teachers and for each other.

"At some point, teachers and parents stopped working together and started working against each other," Ms. Miller says. She says parents and teachers used to work together to advance the best interests of the students, but the relationship between parents and teachers has deteriorated in the past decade.

Without the support of parents, teachers are vulnerable to false claims from students. Students often fabricate complaints about teachers to retaliate against them for disciplinary actions. Administrators are quick to believe the student and don't offer the teacher an opportunity to refute the student's claim. Because students are aware that they can stir up trouble for teachers, they are taking advantage of this power more frequently. Teachers are receiving reprimands, probation, phone calls from social services agencies, and they are being called into court, Ms. Miller says.

"It makes it harder to do my job and to care about going to work when the students are apathetic, and parents are more concerned with being friends with their children than with being parents," she says.

The stress sometimes overwhelms her. To relieve stress, she confides in her friends. Some of them are in the education field and understand, and others are not and are amazed at her stories. "I've also gone to counseling just to have an impartial party to talk to when it has gotten to be too much," she says.

"I'm very fortunate that this year I have an amazing group of students—the complete opposite of what I had last year," she says. She had a few students who started out the year with apathetic attitudes, but she contacted their parents, received supportive responses, and had motivational conversations with the students. By the end of the first quarter, they had turned things around.

"Last year was really the worst year that I had ever had in 11 years of teaching, and I feel renewed this year, mostly due to the group of students I have this year," she says.

* * *

Joan Phillips, Elementary School Teacher, Florida

Joan Phillips has been a teacher for three years. "It's a dream I've always had," she says. Prior to attaining her teaching position at an elementary school in Florida, she was an aide and a teacher's assistant. She has been in the education system for 12 years.

Last year Ms. Phillips had 18 students in her pre-K class, nine regular education students and nine special education students. She says she had positive relationships with most of the parents, and most of her students were well-adjusted and behaved properly. But she had one boy in her class who she sensed had serious emotional problems. He hid in a cubby one day, and she failed to notice until another child pointed it out. She felt the child's parents did not adequately respond to her concerns about their son's behavior.

"I was frustrated with the parents," she says. "When you're trying to help and open the lines of communications, you don't want to get into their personal lives; you just want to be there for the child, but they don't see it that way." She felt the parents were not as attentive to the child's needs as they should be. After the graduation party on the last day of school, all of the parents took their children home, but this little boy's parents left without him. "He freaked out and threw a tantrum," she says.

"I tried to give him as much love as I could in the classroom," she says. She designated him her special helper. After he became upset and refused to get on the bus to an aftercare program at another school, she placed him in her school's aftercare program. The boy was not able to handle change. When she expressed her concerns to the child's parents, they said they would talk to him. But she doesn't know if they ever did.

She didn't think about how the situation made her feel, she just thought about what she needed to do for the well-being of the child. Her job is to make her students feel safe and secure so they can learn, she says. "I have a passion for my job. I love what I do."

* * *

Attitudes

Notably absent from the teachers' top 10 list is a plea for respect from parents. But many of the teachers interviewed for this book expressed dismay at the lack of respect they receive from some parents. Judy White, a middle school English and social studies teacher in New York, says parents will sometimes exhibit a condescending attitude toward her on the telephone. An English teacher at Ms. White's school, Michelle Anderson, attended a parent-teacher conference the sixth grade team scheduled to express their concerns about a student's performance and behavior. The mother asserted that her son was bored and suggested that if Ms. Anderson would sing and dance during her lessons, he would be more engaged.

* * *

Maureen Richards, Elementary School Teacher, New York

Maureen Richards graduated from a college in New York City with a degree in art history. She moved back home to Massachusetts after graduation and hoped to find a job in a museum. She took a job at Bloomingdale's, but wanted to eventually return to New York City where her boyfriend and friends resided. Her boss recommended her for a buyer's training program in New York City; she moved back and entered the program. She stayed with Bloomingdale's for two years before joining Tiffany & Co.

Ms. Richards was less than enthusiastic about her job in the retail industry. "I felt unfulfilled and chained to a computer," she says. But she was engaged to her boyfriend and planning a wedding that she and her fiancé were paying for, so she remained in her job. When Tiffany underwent a restructuring and implemented changes that she felt squelched her creativity, she resigned.

She knew she needed a change, so she began looking into graduate schools. She became interested in the teaching college in New York that her mother attended because it offered a program that would train her to work in the education department of a museum, creating programs for adults and children.

The program required that she begin student-teaching right away. Because she began the program in January, her advisor suggested she volunteer for the remainder of the year before starting her student-teaching in September. Her advisor placed her with an elementary school teacher the advisor knew and had placed other students with in prior years.

"I immediately loved it," she says. "I clicked with the teacher, I loved the school, I felt I had found my calling."

She returned to the school the following year to student teach. When she graduated, she obtained a job there. She eventually taught first grade, fourth grade and fifth grade during her seven years at the school.

The school was progressive and well-respected, and it drew a diverse student body. The year she was hired, she took over a first grade class from a teacher who taught the class in kindergarten and was expected to have the same class for first grade. The parents supported the concept of looping, and they were displeased that their children were placed with a new teacher, particularly a first-year teacher.

Ms. Richards' first year was overwhelming. Her room was a disaster. Her husband took time off of work to come in and help her paint and organize. After she set up her room, things only got worse. After dismissing her students on the first day of school, she shut the door and cried. She felt she had made a big mistake.

"No one sits you down and tells you what you need to do," she says. "They just throw you in there."

The planning overwhelmed her the most. Creating lessons and activities every day was difficult. Math was not as taxing as the other subjects because she was provided with a specific curriculum that she was required to follow. But for the other subjects, she had to create lessons from scratch. The school followed the balanced literacy approach to reading (incorporating whole language and phonics), which required shared reading, guided reading and read-alouds. The school had a reputation for focusing on social studies, and she felt she had to do a thorough job in that subject area.

She didn't find the school's staff developers to be of much help. "Some were good, and some were terrible," she says. "I was completely overwhelmed by how much work it was." She arrived at school between 7 and 7:30 a.m. and stayed until 4 or 5 p.m., planning and setting up her room. She also brought work home with her.

The principal had been at the school for 35 years and expected her staff to do everything a certain way. Even though Ms. Richards was in desperate need of guidance and support, she was reluctant to approach the principal and admit she needed help for fear of making a negative impression. When she encountered behavior problems in her classroom, she refrained from sending students to the office because she felt this was a sign of weakness.

Ms. Richards believes in the importance of parental involvement, but the parents at her school were so involved she found it overwhelming. The administration allowed parents to visit the classrooms for the first half hour of the day and welcomed them to visit the school any time. The parents felt entitled to approach teachers and criticize them at any time.

In her first year teaching fourth grade, the pressure to adequately prepare her students for the state's standardized tests created stress. The day before the Christmas break, she eagerly anticipated her upcoming trip with her husband to the Bahamas. She was in dire need of a vacation. She was walking down the hall on her way to make copies when a parent approached her. The woman blurted out, "I wanted to tell you that my daughter doesn't like you, and she says none of the other kids like you either."

"I was so stunned," Ms. Richards says. The woman didn't make an appointment to discuss her daughter's issues in a parent-teacher conference; she unexpectedly accosted Ms. Richards in the hallway. She responded by telling the woman her comment was vague and asked for elaboration. She asked the woman if her daughter feels her teaching style is too tough, or if perhaps it's too easy. What is it, specifically, that she dislikes, Ms. Richards inquired. But she did not receive a helpful response.

Ms. Richards' vacation was marred by her obsession with the woman's comment. She continued to dwell on it throughout the week. She fretted that the woman would complain to the principal. She talked about it with her husband.

"My husband said if he went home and said to his mother that he didn't like his teacher, his mother would have said, 'Well, what did you do?'" But parents today are "overindulgent" and quick to blame the teacher and the school, she says. The child is not held accountable when problems in school arise.

She entered her classroom after Christmas break feeling miserable. "I tried to put it behind me and dot my i's and cross my t's with this kid. Whenever there was a family conference, I was extremely prepared," she says. But the child was moody and exhibited a negative attitude. The other teachers told Ms. Richards the girl behaved the same way with them, and she probably didn't like anyone. Ms. Richards eventually decided to take the mother's comment with "a grain of salt" and tried to get past it. "It took me a while," she says. "I still remember the story. It had an impact on me."

The incident was not the first time Ms. Richards felt disrespected by a parent. In her first year, a parent visited Ms. Richards' classroom the day the superintendent was scheduled to observe her teaching the class. She was always anxious when the principal or superintendent was expected to observe her, and she worked diligently to prepare impressive lessons. That morning, the visiting parent thoughtlessly placed a wet umbrella on a chart she created for her lesson before the superintendent later that day. When she picked up the chart during the lesson, the marker started to run and the chart began to fall apart. She became flustered and the lesson unraveled. The superintendent flagged her as requiring additional support. She says observations are stressful for teachers, in general, because of the lack of control they have over the situation, particularly with the younger grades. If a child is acting out or feeling sick at the moment, there is nothing the teacher can do.

While teaching first grade, she had an encounter with a parent after she rearranged the students' seats, as teachers periodically do. One mother came in the next day to request Ms. Richards provide the parents and students with advance notice the next time she planned to change the seating assignments to allow them to prepare. Ms. Richards was taken aback by the request. "It's the teacher's prerogative to change seats," she says.

Ms. Richards theorizes that parents who are disrespectful and demanding toward teachers were traumatized in school as young children. In an attempt to recover, they go to extremes to protect their children from negative experiences. They don't want their children to be disappointed or upset. But in their efforts to guard their children against adversity, parents are becoming too indulgent, she says. They are misinterpreting their role in their child's life—they want to be their child's friend, rather than their parent. They want to be liked. "Parents are afraid of their kids," she says. From her point of view, she says this approach to parenting is a mistake because children are not developing a sense of responsibility. School is not only about educating children, but it is also about teaching them to follow rules and respect authority. Parents are losing sight of that goal, she says.

She also speculates that teachers don't command respect because they don't make a lot of money and they work with children. But the most important factor may be that people perceive the teacher's job to be comfortable and easy. "People are bitter about it," she says. They resent that teachers get time off for the summer, school vacations and holidays. "My doorman used to say, 'It's another day off for Maureen,'" she says.

The lack of regard for teachers is also evident in idle conversation, she says. When she tells people at cocktail parties or other social gatherings that she's a teacher, they say, "Oh, that's so cute." Or they say, "I hate fifth graders." And that's the end of the conversation. "It drains the oxygen out of the room," she says. But when she mentions she used to work at Tiffany & Co., she evokes a much different response. "They say, 'Oh, that's so fascinating.'"

If teachers are unable to elicit respect from parents, they have little chance of commanding respect from their students, Ms. Richards says. One first grader called her a "dog-faced bitch." When Ms. Richards sent students to the main office, they would often sit there and color because the principal was too busy to deal with discipline problems. The school had no assistant principal to handle discipline.

The school also lacked an effective policy for dealing with behavior problems. Thus children who exhibited poor behavior did not face consequences.

Behavior management is one of the most difficult aspects of the job, and it cannot be taught in school or in a book, she says. She considers the techniques she was taught to be ineffective in cases of severe discipline problems. Tips such as shut off the lights, ring a bell or clap to get the class' attention often don't work in practice.

One disobedient student can change the whole dynamics of the class, Ms. Richards says. She had a fourth grader who tended to rile the class up. When he was absent, the classroom dynamics changed entirely. He was unable to sit still and pay attention, he would distract the other students with noises mimicking flatulence or with a GI Joe doll in his pocket, and he constantly took bathroom breaks. She taught a fifth grader who would constantly hurt himself; for example, he would intentionally bang his head. She taught a first grader who would suddenly flee from the classroom.

Ms. Richards says her kinship with her colleagues and the strong sense of community at her school helped her cope with the stress and anxiety she experienced. The close-knit, supportive group of teachers worked as a team. Without the camaraderie of her colleagues, "I wouldn't have survived," she says.

Her husband drew a high enough salary to support their family, so she did not experience the anxiety teachers often feel about their finances and the stress they experience from taking on extra work for additional pay. Some of her colleagues were forced to tutor, supervise an after-school activity or take a second job over the summer. She was able to travel during the summer and rejuvenate.

After seven years, Ms. Richards left her job because she had a baby. But she misses teaching and plans to resume her career one day. "I love the dynamics of being the classroom teacher. I love the groove you get into," she says. "You form a family with the kids. I love the energy and all the different personalities. I love how fast-paced the days are. I love opening the door in the morning and seeing the kids running in."

"It made me feel good about myself that I was spending my time in a meaningful way," she says. "For every annoying kid there are many wonderful ones."

* * *

Sandra Hall, High School Teacher, New York

Sandra Hall was an interior designer for 12 years before becoming a teacher. She abandoned the design world because of the long hours. She wanted to have a family, and did not want to be away from home for extended periods of time. She always wanted to pursue a career in the art field, and decided teaching would allow her to work regular hours.

Ms. Hall teaches high school art classes in a New York suburb. She is content with her career decision because she enjoys spending vacations with her children. Three days a week she is able to get home in time to greet them when they come off the school bus.

Parents don't consider art to be as important as the other classes in which their children are enrolled, she says. Still, she makes an effort to communicate with parents about the progress their children are making in her classes. She was concerned about a student who failed to make an effort in class or complete his homework assignments. His lack of effort was affecting his grade. Ms. Hall contacted the student's parents to express her concern. When she spoke with the student's mother, Ms. Hall suggested the student enroll in another art class that was not as intense and did not require homework. The student's mother did not take Ms. Hall's advice, and by the end of the year, the student was barely passing. Ms. Hall called the student's mother again. This time, the mother reacted to Ms. Hall's concerns by belittling the class. She stated, "It's art, for God's sake."

Despite the misconception among some parents that art is not as important as other subjects, Ms. Hall's schedule is just as rigorous as her colleagues' schedules. She teaches five classes and has three prep periods to grade assignments and prepare for class. Sometimes she skips lunch to avoid working after hours, but she is still forced to take work home occasionally. "I have an insane amount of grading," she says. Like other teachers, art teachers are also observed by administrators. She says parents don't realize how often teachers are observed.

The mother of another one of Ms. Hall's students called her on behalf of her daughter to ask for an extension on a project. The project was due the same day as an Advanced Placement exam, which the mother considered a higher priority. Ms. Hall said she could not make an exception for the student. The mother requested Ms. Hall ask the director of the art department for permission to make an exception. The director of the department supported Ms. Hall's decision. The mother was displeased that Ms. Hall refused to accommodate her request. "This is art, not brain surgery," she scoffed.

Ms. Hall has a hard time accepting the attitude parents display toward her class. "I hate it, I absolutely hate it," she says. "But there's nothing I can say to change their minds, so I just say, 'I'm sorry you feel that way.'" She adds, "It bothers me, but in a day or two I forget about it." Fortunately, difficult parents and students are "few and far between," she says. Most of the students are diligent, and most of the parents are appreciative when they receive a phone call from her.

She would prefer that parents call her or request a conference when they have a concern. But most parents e-mail her. Parents have unrealistic expectations when it comes to e-mail, she says. They think teachers are available to respond instantly.

Still, she strives to foster positive relationships with the parents of her students and to impress administrators when she is being observed. She says teachers are keenly aware that everything is written down and placed in their files. If a parent or an administrator is dissatisfied with a teacher's performance, the teacher has to make an effort to rectify the problem so a case cannot be built against him or her.

Chapter Four

Office Politics

"I had already developed a thick skin.
If I was right out of college, I would have died."

Cynthia Collins, Middle School Teacher, California

Administrators

Emma Franklin, Middle School Teacher, Massachusetts

After Emma Franklin graduated from college, she spent more than a year involved in volunteer work in Nicaragua. One of her volunteer jobs entailed teaching English to students attending a new school in the village where she lived. When she returned from Nicaragua, she decided to settle down in Massachusetts. She had attended college in the state, and some of her friends continued to reside there. One of her friends mentioned that she knew of an all-girls Catholic charter school that needed a Spanish teacher. She didn't intend to pursue a career in education, but she needed a job, and the teaching position would give her an opportunity to use her Spanish. She applied for the job, and received an offer.

The charter school was established based upon the premise that the public school system was inadequate, she says. The founders felt they could create a superior educational institution. Their approach was to hire young, recent college graduates who would stay for a year or two and move on. After teaching at the school for two years, she questioned this strategy. She wondered whether a school staffed by a group of inexperienced teachers who lacked certification could be more effective than traditional public schools. She felt she could be a more successful teacher if she obtained the education required to receive teaching credentials from the state. She felt compelled to explore the public school system and the teaching profession. "I felt there was a lot to learn. I wanted to learn," she says.

She entered a free teacher certification program in Los Angeles where she could teach full-time during the day and take classes at night. Her observations contradicted the charter school's assertion that public schools are inadequate. The teachers she met were committed and inspiring. But she watched many teachers come and go. The situation made an impact on her. "Kids deserve more than a revolving door," she says.

She also discovered something about herself while teaching in Los Angeles. "I was good at it," she says. "And it was stimulating to me; I loved it." She decided to pursue a career as a teacher.

She taught seventh and eighth grade English in Los Angeles for a total of three years before returning to Massachusetts to attain a master's degree. During that time, she held a year-long internship at a middle school, which ultimately hired her to teach English.

In her first year teaching in the middle school, she was given an inclusion humanities (English and history) class by mistake. Early on, she suspected her class was an inclusion class (an inclusion class includes students who are entitled to special education services in accordance with their individual education plans). But when she approached the administration with her concerns, she was told that she was being too judgmental.

Ms. Franklin did not have a special education degree, and the school lacked support personnel—such as a psychologist or guidance counselor—who could help her address the special needs of the children in her class. She couldn't consult her colleagues because none of them knew the children well enough. She had the most interaction with the students because she taught both English and history. The students went to science only every other day, and the math teacher was a substitute. The school hired a regular math teacher in October, but he was ineffective and left at the end of the year.

In addition to the students who appeared to have learning disabilities, a few of the students had more serious issues. One of the students entered the class each day screaming, "I'm not reading." She soon discovered the student was unable to read. She expressed her concerns to the vice principal, who advised trying to relate to the student better. The vice principal said the boy had an interest in basketball, and she suggested Ms. Franklin try bonding with him by talking about the sport. Ms. Franklin knew the problem was not her inability to connect with the student. She suspected his issues were more serious than the vice principal was willing to acknowledge. She had weekly conversations with the boy's sister, who was in her 30s and helping to raise him. His grandmother had legal custody. The sister was also concerned about the boy. The student was eventually evaluated and determined to have mental retardation.

Another student in Ms. Franklin's class appeared to have a mental illness. She kept hearing voices. She heard noises behind her and would blurt out, "Who's touching me?" when nobody was near her. When the other students turned to look at her, she would complain, "Why is everyone looking at me?" Another girl was "smart and very sweet" but appeared to have something "off" about her, Ms. Franklin says. She called the student's home one night to speak to her mother, and the student answered the phone. The girl said her mother wasn't there, and she didn't know where her mother was; she sounded distressed. Ms. Franklin called back several times. The final time the girl was hysterical and could barely speak. Ms. Franklin called the vice principal, who went to the girl's house. Ms. Franklin found out the next day that the girl had been molested by a family member, and her mother had been talking about an upcoming visit from the relative. The girl was concerned about her younger sister.

Meanwhile, Ms. Franklin's observations continued to fuel her suspicions that some of her students had learning disabilities that were not being addressed. Because the school administration ignored her concerns, she accessed her students' records on her own and found that most of them did have individual education plans. She presented this evidence to the administrators, who finally acknowledged that a mistake was made—the special education teacher was given the regular education class and Ms. Franklin, who does not have a special education degree, was given the inclusion class. Still, the administration refused to rectify the situation, maintaining that Ms. Franklin would probably do a better job teaching the students because the special education teacher was unhappy and apathetic.

Ms. Franklin called a couple of parents who she knew would complain if they were aware of the situation. She told them that their children were not receiving the services they were entitled to because they were placed in the wrong class. Ultimately, the administration resolved the problem by bringing the special education teacher in to co-teach the inclusion class with Ms. Franklin. A new teacher was hired to take over the regular education class. But the changes did not take place until January.

While the issue she faced in her classroom was addressed, she felt the school's overall structure was flawed. She believed she could not be an effective, successful teacher in the school's current environment. She felt the school should have a team of teachers at each grade level who knew the students well and collaborated together. The students needed to feel as though their teachers knew them, understood them and supported them. A deeper connection with their teachers was essential for them to feel motivated to achieve.

Feeling disillusioned, she considered quitting and looked into other jobs. She eventually decided to try to initiate changes at her school to dismantle the barriers to success. She and a friend, a seventh grade teacher, hammered out a plan and proposed it to the principal. After reviewing the proposal, the principal gave the teachers the go-ahead to implement their plan.

The teacher who co-developed the plan with Ms. Franklin moved up from seventh grade to teach eighth grade math. They separated English and history and took part in the process of hiring a new history teacher. They adopted a team approach in which the teachers would collaborate on how best to address the needs of each student. Ms. Franklin was the only teacher who assigned homework previously; now all of the teachers were expected to assign homework. Students who did not complete their homework were required to stay after school and finish their assignments in the new study hall Ms. Franklin and her colleague established.

The year the changes were implemented, Ms. Franklin taught a regular education class, and the school hired a new special education teacher for the inclusion class. But for the past two years, she has co-taught an inclusion class with a special education teacher and finds the experience rewarding.

She has been teaching in the middle school for five years and continues to find her workload overwhelming. She invests a considerable amount of time and effort into lesson planning and grading. She says she could not be an effective teacher otherwise. In her first year, she took a personal day to stay home and grade papers for her 150 students from 7 a.m. until 7 p.m. She acknowledges that not all teachers spend the kind of time she does on preparation and grading, and notes that they are paid the same salary that she is, or more if they have been at the school longer.

Ms. Franklin says she has worked with apathetic teachers who present a negative image of the teaching profession. She has worked with teachers who polish their nails during class or take time off to audition for acting jobs. The English teacher who was assigned to be her mentor in Los Angeles managed to avoid teaching most of the year by having the class listen to opera music or listen to him play the xylophone. "When he finally got around to teaching, he would tell stories about himself," she says.

Another colleague in Los Angeles sexually harassed Ms. Franklin's students, commenting on their clothing or appearance. He made comments to Ms. Franklin's teaching assistant and pressured her in front of the class to accept a date with him, causing her to feel uncomfortable. Ms. Franklin complained about his behavior to the principal and faced a backlash from the other male teachers, who made her the object of jokes. She says the episode eventually blew over and the teacher left the school.

Ms. Franklin often spends six hours on a Saturday or four hours on a Friday night in planning sessions with other teachers. She feels the time she invests in collaborating with other teachers is not valued by the administration because it's not expected or visible. Administrators tend to recognize and value the time teachers spend chaperoning field trips or serving as a student club advisor because those efforts are more noticeable.

Much of her time is spent addressing the unrealistic demands of administrators. "I feel professionally disrespected constantly," she says. "It's ridiculous." She was told to change rooms three times in one year, often on short notice. She has had to move her entire classroom herself to a different room or a different building. One summer some of her colleagues were told to move their rooms before school started. They were forced to move while they were still on summer vacation, and they were given one week's notice. When she has had to move her classroom, she didn't have a child and was able to drop everything to move. She had a baby last year and is finding it difficult to balance work and family.

When Ms. Franklin was nine months pregnant, the principal asked the assistant principal to organize the school's book room. Ms. Franklin was informed by a custodian that a pile of books, many of them classics, were lying in the dumpster. She frantically ran around the building enlisting the help of other teachers to rescue the books from the garbage. She later surveyed the books spread across the conference room table and realized the task of organizing them would fall on her.

* * *

Carol Wright, Middle School Teacher, New York

Carol Wright taught sixth, seventh and eighth grade math at a Catholic school in New York City. Because she took initiative and demonstrated that she was responsible, the school principal began to rely on her extensively. Ms. Wright was expected to handle many of the principal's responsibilities, such as running the staff meetings and evaluating the other teachers. The principal asked Ms. Wright to conduct a practice Mass for the students. The principal did not keep track of the number of days the teachers worked during the year, so she relied on Ms. Wright's personal calendar.

In Ms. Wright's fourth year at the school, she requested a move to fourth grade. She hoped the experience would help her gain a position at a suburban elementary school. The principal accidentally gave Ms. Wright the fifth grade social studies textbooks, and gave the fifth grade teacher the fourth grade social studies textbooks. Because it was her first year teaching fourth grade, Ms. Wright didn't realize the mistake and used the wrong book the entire year. "We were lucky we had books, I guess," she says.

* * *

Parents

In addition to reporting to the school principal and other administrators, teachers are also responsible to parents. An elementary school teacher can have anywhere from 20 to 35 students in a class, which means forging relationships with up to 70 parents. Middle school and high school teachers interact with an even larger group of parents. For example, if a middle or high school teacher has six classes per day with 25 students in each class, they are in contact with 150 sets of parents.

* * *

Judy White, Middle School Teacher, New York

Judy White always wanted to be a teacher. "I love learning," she says. "I worked hard in school. I come from a disadvantaged background, but I always tried my hardest." Despite her aspirations, her family couldn't afford to send her to college. She had no choice but to find a job after she graduated from high school. Yet she naturally settled into the role of mentor and teacher in her jobs and in her life. People gravitated to her when they needed help and advice. She sensed she had an affinity for teaching. "This is what you're meant to do," she told herself.

Ms. White held a variety of jobs. She cleaned houses, worked in retail sales, cleaned carpets and managed a health club, among other things. It wasn't until she was in her 30s and her children were in school that her ambitions of becoming a teacher were reignited. She had been working as a classroom aide for two years when the school principal encouraged her to go back to school to become a teacher. She told him she needed to work to help support her family. He said he would help her.

The principal put her on the list of substitute teachers so she could earn extra money. She continued to work as an aide in addition to working as a substitute. She went to school at night to obtain her teaching credentials, and she graduated with a 4.0 grade point average. "That was a defining moment," she says. "I didn't think I could do it."

She was hired as a teaching assistant for a first grade class in the school where she worked as an aide. It was an "open" classroom environment with two classes in two adjoined rooms. The two teachers had a total of 40 students. When a child misbehaved, it was Ms. White's duty to walk the child to the principal's office. One boy, in particular, was reprimanded constantly for choking the other children. Because the classroom was spacious, he was able to find a remote corner where he would attack a classmate.

Ms. White asked the boy why he engaged in this behavior. He responded that he was hungry. He said he choked the other children because they had good, healthy snacks and lunches and he had junk food. He said he didn't eat breakfast and had cheese doodles for dinner. Ms. White related the boy's story to the principal. They took off the boy's shirt and saw that he was emaciated.

From that point on, the teachers made sure he ate. They made him oatmeal in the school kitchen before school started in the morning. They got an extra sandwich from the cafeteria and sent it home with him at the end of the day.

At the end of that year, the children made thank you cards for Ms. White. The boy's card said, "I want to thank you for getting me food."

"It was so powerful that you could make that kind of a difference," she says. The experience taught her how important it is for teachers to make a connection with each of their students.

"If you can't make a personal connection with a kid, you can't teach them," she says. Her experience growing up in a lower-income neighborhood helps her relate to students from diverse backgrounds. "I'm very accepting and I don't go in with any preconceived notions." She also shares stories about herself to help break down her students' defenses. "I'm not guarded," she says. She has told her students about the time in seventh grade when she wet her pants because someone threw her in the bushes. She has told them that she cheated on a biology test and that experience stays with her. She feels her stories help her students relate to her and enable them to see her as a real person. She also maintains a sense of humor and is not afraid to laugh at herself.

Ms. White currently teachers English and social studies in a middle school in an affluent suburb in New York. Despite the abundance of resources available to teachers in her district, she says the privileged children she teaches are harder to reach than children from middle class areas. "We have everything we need to do our jobs, but it's not any easier," she says of her upper class school district. She teaches some students with serious emotional issues, she says. "It's harder for the kids to trust you."

The beginning of the year is the hardest because she hasn't made any personal connections with the students yet. But she makes an effort to learn about her students and to ascertain what works for each one of them. Her abilities in this area have improved over the years, she says. The process starts with observing the students closely. She allows them to choose their own seats, and she watches to see who they sit with. She tries to determine their social structure—who are the power players, who are the loners. Teachers who assign seats are eliminating an important source of information about their students and who they are, she says. "I let kids be the first couple of days."

She strives to understand each child and to treat her students as individuals—as human beings—not just as students of the subjects she teaches. "You don't teach a subject, you teach children," she says.

It can be emotionally difficult for teachers, particularly younger teachers, to confront the personal problems their students face. "When you're young and new at teaching, you do bring it home and lose sleep, but I have learned that there's a limit. I do have to pass on some of the responsibility," she says. "As I've gotten older, I've learned to reach out to parents. Because I'm older, parents are more receptive to what I have to say."

Ms. White calls all of her students' parents (she had 126 last year) in the fall to establish the foundation of a relationship. Through these connections, she learns important information about the child's home life and family that may affect his or her performance and behavior in class. Last year she found out three of her students had parents battling cancer. She has found out that parents are going through a divorce or that they have a mixed marriage. She would not have known any of this information if she did not make that initial phone call, she says. More important, her phone calls start her relationships with the parents on a positive path and avert problems that may arise later in the year.

She has noticed that younger teachers are often judgmental of parents and sometimes have difficulty working with them. "I say, 'Until you've walked a mile in their shoes, you don't know that life and you can't judge them.'"

But she acknowledges that she has had confrontations with parents herself. Sometimes when younger teachers are having trouble with a parent, Ms. White will volunteer to call the parent on behalf of the staff. She recalls one parent who was particularly difficult for all of the teachers to deal with. "She made our lives hell." Ms. White finally told the parent, "Just because you went to school, doesn't make you a teacher." She went on to inform the parent that she has been successfully teaching 11-year-olds for years, and she knows what she's doing. She asked the parent to let go a little and trust her. "I have to put them in their place. I don't pussyfoot around. I'm a hard ass," she says.

Although she's firm with parents, she remains professional and respectful, and asks parents to do the same. Sometimes fathers will call her and talk to her like they talk to their secretaries at their high-powered jobs, she says. "I say, 'Hold it. Don't talk to me that way. It's disrespectful. I understand that you're upset, but we have to be professional here.'" Sometimes she suggests discontinuing the conversation and meeting in person for a conference. "They come in more rational."

The advent of the cell phone has made life more difficult for teachers, Ms. White contends. "The cell phone is not a friend to the teacher," she says. Oftentimes, a student who becomes upset because he or she just received a poor grade or dealt with another problem will immediately call his or her parent, prompting the parent to become irate and call the teacher. Such situations would be less volatile if the student would wait until he or she arrived home to discuss the issue because the intense emotions that swell up initially often dissipate in time.

E-mail also creates problems because parents have a tendency to write things in an e-mail that they wouldn't say verbally—things that are often inappropriate. Furthermore, parents expect an immediate response from teachers. They "expect you to jump," she says. "We don't have jobs like you. We're not at a desk. You may have left for the day by the time I get back to you," she says.

Voice mail, on the other hand, gives a teacher time to consider his or her response to a parent's message. If a younger colleague receives a voice mail message from a parent, Ms. White suggests the teacher talk it through with a colleague or mentor before returning the call.

She advises the teacher to do some fact-finding by touching base with the child and talking to other colleagues or the guidance office. Often the problem can be resolved before the call is returned. A teacher should never call a parent back immediately without taking the time to formulate an appropriate response, Ms. White says, adding that she has been caught off guard by parents in the past.

She also suggests to her colleagues that they never meet with parents alone. "Parents turn things around sometimes. You don't always know what you're up against," she says. She encourages her younger colleagues to rely on their support staff—administrators, guidance counselors and colleagues. "Younger teachers don't know how to share the burden," she says. "It's emotionally draining." Sometimes new teachers are reluctant to approach administrators or colleagues for help because they don't want to give the impression they are having difficulty, fearing this may reflect poorly on their job performance and affect their chances of obtaining tenure. "They walk a fine line," she says.

Ms. White also has advice for parents who want to play a positive role in their children's educations. She suggests they get involved with the school, attend PTA meetings and stay connected.

* * *

Marie Young, Elementary School Teacher, California

Marie Young has been teaching kindergarten at the same school for nine years. She says many parents seek positive relationships with her and offer their assistance whenever possible. With others, she senses a lack of confidence and trust, which is stressful. She is apprehensive about disciplining those students, and she is nervous at parent-teacher conferences and chooses her words carefully. "Parents can really make or break your year," she says.

She had a student in her class who stepped on a ladybug in the classroom after she asked him to leave it alone. The action resulted in the student's clip being moved from green to yellow—denoting a demerit. [Ms. Young's clip system works as follows: Each child has a clip that is similar to a paper clip or clothespin. Every day, the students start their clips on green. If a child breaks a rule, he or she receives a warning. If the student breaks another rule, the child's clip is moved to yellow, which means another warning. If he or she continues to break a rule, the clip is moved to orange and the student must take an orange card home to be signed by a parent. The card explains the rule that was broken. If the behavior continues, the clip moves to red and the child takes a red card home. The clip is immediately moved to red if the child is guilty of a major infraction, such as hitting, kicking or pushing. If the child stays on green or yellow, the child takes home a green card at the end of the day. When the child receives ten green cards, he or she returns them for a small prize.]

After hearing about the ladybug incident, the student's mother approached Ms. Young and asked her what happened. Ms. Young told her. A few days later, the mother asked Ms. Young if she could come into the class to volunteer. The mother had never volunteered before, and when she came to the class, Ms. Young got the impression she was there mainly to observe her. This was not the first time a parent offered to volunteer but was primarily interested in checking up on Ms. Young. She comes to this conclusion when the parent is not interested in working with the children and just sits in the back of the room doing paperwork. "They're watching to see what you're going to say and how you're interacting with their child," she says.

She doesn't mind parents coming into the class to observe her, but their attitude toward her does create stress. "I want to make the parents happy," she says.

While most of the parents she works with are supportive, others convey a lack of respect for her abilities. She wonders why people consider their doctors to be experts and don't question their advice, but they don't exhibit the same respect for teachers. She often feels like telling parents, "Just let me do my job; I know what I'm doing."

A parent's lack of faith in a teacher's professional opinion can work against the child's best interest, she says. In her second year of teaching, two children who had autism were added to her roster, which was already full at 20. The students were originally assigned to the self-contained special education class. But the parents requested the school mainstream the children, against the special education teacher's recommendation. Ms. Young understood the parents' motivation and knew they were just doing what they thought was best for their children. But, acknowledging her limitations, she felt placing the children in her class would not benefit them. She did not have a special education degree and was not equipped to adequately address their needs.

One couple filed a lawsuit demanding their child receive services beyond what their child was already receiving; for example, they wanted all of the students in the class to receive adaptive physical education to avoid placing their child in a special class, and they wanted two of the students in the class to join their child in speech therapy to serve as role models. While Ms. Young was sympathetic to the parents' need to advocate for their child, she felt the child would benefit more from the special education class. The issue was settled in mediation with the school district meeting the parents' demands. Instead of fighting for what was best for the child, the school district was forced to accommodate the parents to avoid incurring any further costs.

"It was disheartening to watch the process go on and know this was not what was best for them," she says.

She had no special education training, and the students' one-to-one aides lacked college degrees. "As a new teacher, it was very stressful," she says. One of the students was keenly interested in computers, and was preoccupied during circle time by the computer situated behind Ms. Young. To avoid the distraction, she switched the set-up of her room and put the computer behind the students during circle time. She placed a screen in front of the computer to completely conceal it from view. She did not anticipate that the change would upset the student, not realizing that autistic children have difficulty adjusting to change. The student continued to face in the same direction he was accustomed to, but now he had his back to Ms. Young. At the same time she was trying to figure out how to accommodate the autistic children, Ms. Young had to deal with the typical issues the rest of the kindergarteners had, such as bathroom accidents.

She has faced situations in which parents were disrespectful for reasons that had nothing to do with her teaching ability. She was summoned to the principal's office one year because a student's father was there complaining that she did not say hello to him in the hallway earlier that week. He demanded to confront all of the kindergarten teachers because he did not know Ms. Young's name. Irate, he accused Ms. Young of being disrespectful for failing to acknowledge him in the hallway. She apologized, saying that she didn't see him in the hallway or she would have greeted him.

After the confrontation in the principal's office, Ms. Young was distraught the remainder of the day. She tried to tell herself that there must be something else bothering the man because most people wouldn't get so upset over such a minor incident. But she still internalized the situation. The following week, the student transferred to a different school. She is not sure whether there were other issues involved in that decision.

* * *

Amy Roberts, Middle School Teacher, New York

Amy Roberts' mother was a teacher, and she attended the school where her mother worked. She liked her mother's schedule because it allowed them to spend time together after school and during the summer. After graduating from college, where she majored in psychology, she attended graduate school to obtain her teacher certification and a master's degree. She has been teaching at an elementary school in a New York suburb for 11 years. She is looking forward to having her daughter go to school where she teaches.

Ms. Roberts taught third grade for two years at a Catholic school in New York City before accepting a position at her current school. She taught fourth grade for two years and has been teaching fifth grade for nine years.

She enjoys working with children, especially fourth and fifth graders, and she likes how teaching relates to her psychology major. But working with children can be difficult because they have different boundaries than adults, she says. Teachers have to carefully monitor what they say and how they behave because they never know how their students will interpret their actions.

Ms. Roberts recalls an incident when she sent a student to the principal's office for constantly disrupting her class. Shortly after, she visited the office to deal with a separate issue, and the secretary suggested she participate in the principal's discussion with the student while she was there. During the conversation in the principal's office, the student kept referring to Ms. Roberts as "she" in a disrespectful manner. The principal leaned in close to the student and firmly told him to show Ms. Roberts respect by referring to her properly. Ms. Roberts says it was fortunate she was there to witness the conversation because the boy told his mother that the principal struck him, even though the principal never touched him. The mother filed charges. When the district attorney looked into the matter to decide whether the mother had a case, Ms. Roberts had to go to the district attorney's office to recount what happened in the principal's office that day. The principal was never charged.

Ms. Roberts had a girl in her class who showed up to school one day with a mark on her cheek that resembled a handprint. She did not suspect abuse and knew there must be another reason for the mark. She jokingly said to the student, "What happened, did you get hit at home?" The student told her mother that Ms. Roberts implied the girl was abused. The mother complained to the vice principal. The vice principal asked Ms. Roberts what happened, and she explained.

When parents have a complaint, they typically go over the teacher's head to an administrator, such as the principal or vice principal, she says. Occasionally they will contact the superintendent or a school board member. The prevalence of e-mail makes it easy for parents to contact any official they choose. Teachers do not always have an opportunity to defend themselves. Even though Ms. Roberts was given the chance to explain her comment to the student, she was upset that the girl's mother put her in that position. She decided to write a letter to the woman explaining that if she had truly suspected abuse she would have reported it, as she is legally bound to do. Writing the letter and standing up for herself made her feel better. The parent did not raise the issue again.

Over the years, Ms. Roberts has become more adept at standing up for herself to parents, and she finds it helps her cope with distressing situations. When she had a conflict with a parent earlier in her career, she would cry and feel miserable for a few days until she got over the upsetting incident.

She also protects her emotional well-being by leaving problems at school. She always contacts parents during school hours. She says she needs a buffer between school and her personal life to deal with the stress.

But the rewards of teaching children make the unpleasant incidents more bearable, she says. She has learned how to relate better to her students. She has high expectations for her students and constantly pushes them to do better. But she also lavishes them with praise. "The more you love them, the more they want to please you," she says. She is strict, but in a nurturing way.

Ms. Roberts also enjoys working with her colleagues. "Working with people who are similar to you is easier," she says. "I find that teachers are very often cut from the same cloth." But one of the toughest aspects of her job is her superintendent's lack of leadership skills and his inability to command respect from the teaching staff. He devised and considered a plan to move teachers around, but instead of gathering the affected teachers together at one time to communicate the changes, he told them separately. When a teacher would leave his office, he or she would tell a colleague about the changes, sparking rumors to tear quickly through the building until the staff was in an uproar. The teachers feel he doesn't make an effort to get to know them and understand their jobs. Their lack of respect for him makes it difficult to accept his decisions. He comes across as a businessman who is more concerned with finances than with education. The previous superintendent made an effort to get to know the teachers in the district, had high expectations for them and commanded respect and loyalty.

* * *

Christina Campbell, High School Teacher, New Jersey

Christina Campbell taught high school science in New Jersey for one year before leaving the position for a job at a consulting firm. She enjoyed mentoring children but faced difficultly dealing with parents. Parents expected her to call them regularly to keep them apprised of their children's progress, even though they received regular progress reports and report cards. She says it was impossible for her to comply with their requests because she had 100 students. She had one student who received two poor test grades, and the parents asked her why she didn't notify them sooner that he was having trouble.

Working with children was also difficult because they interpret language and behavior differently from adults, she says. "Anything you say, a mean look, could emotionally destroy them," she says. She knows she has a sarcastic personality and monitored her words carefully.

Ms. Campbell left her teaching position after one year because she wanted a job that was more closely related to the subject she studied in college, engineering. But she was also looking for more financial compensation. As a teacher, she worked before school, during lunch and after school, and felt the compensation was inadequate. "It's an overworked and underpaid industry," she says of teaching. She opposes the approach to teacher compensation because it's not merit-based but tied to the number of years on the job. The salary structure offers no financial incentive to be successful and no financial penalty for being unsuccessful, she says.

She became a teacher after college because it seemed like a good option at the time. She had been a camp counselor and a tutor, and she enjoyed working with children. But the job is more rigorous and the hours more extensive than most people realize, she says. She arrived at school at 7 a.m. and didn't leave until 4 or 5 p.m. "You have the summers off, but if you don't spend half the summer planning, you're not going to be an effective teacher."

* * *

The Classroom Pressure Cooker

When demanding parents receive unconditional support from the school principal, the dynamic can create an intense environment for teachers. A strained relationship with the school principal is particularly difficult for a teacher to endure when he or she works with colleagues who are unsupportive or adversarial. Teachers in this situation consider the atmosphere of their school buildings to be more politically charged than private companies where they have worked.

A teacher is evaluated on a regular basis by many people—students, parents, administrators and colleagues—and if he or she disappoints, fails to impress or irritates just one of them, his or her job could be in jeopardy. Nearly every state has a law that protects a teacher's job—after a probationary period, the teacher cannot be fired unless a legitimate reason exists, typically related to serious misconduct or job performance. The term for this job protection varies by state and includes tenure, continuing contract status, career status, nonprobationary status and permanent status. The probationary period generally varies from two to five years. Although such laws make it more difficult to discharge a teacher, job security is not guaranteed.

While teachers may have job security to a degree, they cannot get settled into their positions because they could be moved to different grade levels or schools to accommodate increasing or declining enrollment. When Danielle Wilson completed her second year teaching kindergarten at an elementary school in California, she was feeling comfortable in her school and confident about her job. She looked forward to starting her third year. However, due to a drop in enrollment in another grade level, the district shifted teachers around. A teacher with seniority decided she wanted to teach kindergarten and took over Ms. Wilson's position. Ms. Wilson was forced to change schools and move to first grade. While she was disappointed at being uprooted, other teachers were less fortunate—they were informed that they may not have jobs the following year. "It's never really a steady thing from year to year," Ms. Wilson says. Despite the sense of instability from one year to the next, she finds her job rewarding, enjoys working with the children in her class, and says the parents and faculty are supportive.

While Ms. Wilson's experience with the parents and staff at her school has been positive, other teachers say they need the job protection state laws provide because of the many people who have the power to influence the status of their jobs.

Sarah Brown, a middle school teacher in New York, says she has overheard students proudly claiming responsibility for the firing of a non-tenured teacher at her school. She has also overheard students talking about their desire to get certain teachers fired because they harbored animosity toward those teachers.

Barbara Martin, a former guidance counselor at a California elementary school, says she often fielded complaints from parents. "I had parents lining up at my door to complain about teachers, curriculum, homework, staff and other students." Many parents requested the school move their child to another class because they didn't like a particular student in the current class. "As a counselor, I'm trying to teach kids conflict-resolution skills, yet there are parents demanding that the problem be solved by moving the kid," she says. Ms. Martin says she wasted many hours in meetings with parents explaining to them why it isn't a good idea for children to move classrooms every time a concern arises. Yet parents continued to demand she move their child to a different classroom and threatened to call the superintendent if she didn't.

Some parents at Ms. Martin's school aggressively campaigned

against teachers they didn't like, going so far as to spread "vicious rumors" about them. "I watched a very good teacher become so demoralized by one parent's rumors and accusations that her class did become unruly and disorganized." One parent wrote a lengthy letter to the principal, accusing a teacher and Ms. Martin of a host of misdeeds, ranging from neglect to harassment.

Teachers are evaluated almost daily by parents based on feedback from their children; their own interaction with the teacher via e-mail, telephone, written notes and conferences; and their assessments of the homework teachers assign and the grades they award. In addition, teachers are scrutinized by school district personnel. The school principal, district superintendent and school board all evaluate a teacher's performance on a regular basis. Principals and superintendents regularly observe and evaluate teachers in the classroom. School board members may also visit the classroom on occasion.

* * *

Cynthia Collins, Middle School Teacher, California

Cynthia Collins' mother is a teacher, but she never considered pursuing a career in teaching. She didn't think she would enjoy teaching. She never liked school. "Why would I become a teacher?"

she thought. "They don't get any respect."

After graduating from college, Ms. Collins tried different jobs, but they didn't really interest her. After working at a technology consulting firm for five or six years, she accepted a position at a dot-com start-up. The company went under and she found herself out of a job. She needed to find a source of income quickly because she and her husband had just bought a house. She started working as a substitute teacher because the position afforded her the flexibility to job hunt. She could accept teaching assignments on the days when she did not have job interviews. She never intended teaching to be a permanent vocation. She didn't think she would be good at it.

The experience surprised her. "I really loved it," she says. "I thought, if I can enjoy my job, that would be cool." She connected with the kids and found she had an affinity for teaching.

She decided to go back to school to obtain her teaching credentials. "It was not easy," she says. She had to invest time, money and energy into going back to school and training as a student-teacher. But she was committed to her goal.

She landed a job teaching middle school in a reputable school district in an affluent California community. The administration was interested in her because she was older and already had some work experience, while most of the other teachers were right out of college.

The office politics she encountered at the school were worse than anything she had experienced in the business world. Her colleagues and administrators did not offer assistance or support when she started. "They didn't tell me anything," she says. "I didn't know where the faculty lounge was for four months." Nobody introduced her to anyone, she had no mentors, and she was pretty much left to fend for herself.

Ms. Collins was also surprised by how the school principal conducted himself. At her previous jobs, managers maintained a high degree of professionalism when interacting with employees. They didn't want to give an employee a reason to lodge a complaint against them with the human resources department. Her principal, however, behaved amateurishly, lacked the ability to manage people and cultivated a competitive atmosphere among the staff.

Backstabbing was common within the teaching staff, Ms. Collins maintains. "It's one of the nastiest places I've ever worked," she says. The atmosphere was foreign to her. In her previous jobs, she formed friendships, enjoyed socializing with co-workers and always got along with her bosses.

But she was able to handle the situation because of her previous experience in the business world. "I had already developed a thick skin," she says. "If I was right out of college, I would have died." She says it was a "sink or swim" situation, and many of the other teachers sank and left.

Her enthusiasm for her job kept her motivated despite the unpleasant work environment. "I loved being in the classroom," she says. "I had to remind myself I loved the classroom."

She particularly enjoyed the ESL (English as a second language) class she was assigned her first year. She connected with the students and developed a rapport with their families. She was so enthusiastic about the class that she visited the families' homes for conferences if they didn't drive. Even though she felt it was necessary to meet face-to-face with parents, she was reprimanded for visiting their homes. She still looks back on the class with fondness. "To this day, I love those kids," she says. One of her former students recently had a baby and called her from the hospital.

After two years of teaching at the school, she thought she was performing well and was on track to receive tenure. She had paid her dues by teaching five different subjects at different grade levels and was hoping to focus on sixth grade language arts and history in her third year. But the principal handed her a schedule that was completely scattered, yet again. Disappointed with her schedule, she approached the principal to ask him if she could focus on teaching sixth grade. He informed her that 2,000 candidates apply for teaching positions at the school each year and advised her to be happy she had a job.

"It was a slap in the face," she says. "I didn't even come in confrontational." He also warned her, "You're not tenured yet, and you better watch yourself."

The principal indicated in Ms. Collins' review that she didn't collaborate with the other sixth grade teachers. He said the other sixth grade teachers informed him that she refused to sit with them at lunch while they collaborate. He failed to acknowledge that she had a different lunch period than the rest of the sixth grade teachers due to her erratic schedule. Ms. Collins believes one of the sixth grade teachers told the principal Ms. Collins was uncooperative because the teacher wanted her friend to obtain the position that Ms. Collins was pursuing.

She broke down and cried during the meeting with the principal, which is uncharacteristic; she had never lost her composure in front of a manager before. Not only were his comments degrading, but also they were unexpected. She had never received any feedback at all from him previously. She heard that he measured a teacher's success based on the quantity of parent complaints. The parents liked Ms. Collins, so she thought she was meeting his expectations. In addition, she had demonstrated her dedication to her career by pursuing double master's degrees in educational technology and ESL at night.

She left the principal's office feeling disheartened. But in another unexpected move, the principal suddenly gave her the schedule she requested about a month after the confrontation in his office.

Ms. Collins' assessment of her principal is that he's more interested in pleasing parents than in teaching students. The teachers all seem unhappy and stressed out because they work in an atmosphere of fear. The community is so tight that one misstep can bury a teacher. "You do one thing wrong, parents talk, and you're done," she says.

She acknowledges that the parents can be difficult to deal with. "They're in your face constantly, and they sometimes treat you like you work for them," she says. But she understands that half the job is working with parents because she believes educating children should be a team effort. "You do need the parents' buy-in," she says. Developing a productive relationship with the parent results in the optimal academic experience for the child, she says. She has a two-year-old daughter, and she feels that being a parent allows her to relate to the parents and to understand their points of view regarding their children.

But even before she became a mother, she says she was adept at working with parents because she was accustomed to working with clients in her previous jobs. "They are clients and you have to make them happy," she says.

To strengthen her relationships with parents, Ms. Collins invites parent volunteers to her classroom every Friday. She believes parents should step back more when their children reach middle school, but many of them "can't let go." The volunteer program allows parents to maintain the closeness with their children that they seek, and they appreciate the opportunity to be involved with the class. It also benefits Ms. Collins because they can watch her in action and get to know her. This irritates her colleagues, she says.

Ms. Collins has established a solid reputation as a structured, tough-love teacher with high expectations and successful results. "When I discipline the kids, it's out of love," she says. "Parents see I love my job and care about their kids." Parents also like her because she's flexible. She'll grant a student an extension for a legitimate reason, but expects the work to meet her high standards when it is turned in.

Although Ms. Collins has a good reputation and develops positive relationships with most parents, she has still had some unpleasant experiences. One year, she offered her students the choice of taking a test the Friday before a three-day weekend or the Tuesday after, which happened to be the day after Halloween. Many of the students wanted the three-day weekend to study and opted to take the test on Tuesday. After the exam on Tuesday, one of the parents e-mailed her a four-paragraph poem titled, "The Grinch That Stole Halloween," and nothing more. She was impressed by how well-written the poem was, even though it was hostile, she says. She replied to the e-mail by calmly explaining her offer to the students, but she signed her e-mail "The Grinch." She didn't receive a response from the parent. The episode concerned her because the mother was a power player in the community. "She was an influential person, so you get nervous," Ms. Collins says. But she later heard the woman shared the poem with other parents, who supported Ms. Collins. "The parents were like, 'Why did you do that?'"

Ms. Collins experiences anguish when she witnesses students behaving cruelly to one another. A beautiful and popular girl in her class tormented an autistic boy. The boy tended to stare at the girl, and she claimed he was looking at her inappropriately. Ms. Collins saw her hike up her shorts to tease him. The girl placed a note in his backpack asking him to meet her at a designated spot. She wrote a similar note to another girl in the class, signed it from a popular boy, and dropped it in the other girl's backpack. When the other girl and the autistic boy showed up at the same place, the girl who instigated the meeting took pictures and circulated them. Ultimately, the autistic boy was asked to leave the school. His parents hired a lawyer and protested. Ms. Collins went with the parents and supported them at the school board meeting.

When faced with disturbing situations, Ms. Collins goes home at the end of the day feeling miserable and cries. But then she will receive a positive e-mail from a parent, and she remembers there are other students in her class who make the job enjoyable and rewarding. When she was going through the harrowing situation with the autistic student, she wrote down the names of five students who were performing well in her class and called their parents to let them know. She needed something positive to lift herself out of her misery.

Ms. Collins has been at her school for five years now, and expects to remain there for the foreseeable future, despite her frustrations. She has considered changing schools, and has even applied for other positions outside of the district, but she always decides to stay. She enjoys teaching her students and is getting to know the parents. She won the district's Teacher of the Year award last year after receiving the nomination from the students and parents. She doesn't relish the idea of starting over in another school where she will have to build her reputation again. Most importantly, she now lives in the community where she teaches, and her daughter will attend her school. She is also pleased with the compensation she receives.

Although Ms. Collins faces a handful of emotionally devastating experiences each year, she tries not to let them squelch her enthusiasm and positive attitude toward her job. "I have to keep reminding myself that there is so much more good than bad," she says.

***

Kim Thompson, Elementary School Teacher, New York

Kim Thompson was a good student until the seventh grade, when she stopped going to class to hang out with her friends, smoke and play video games. She was having problems at home with her family, and her self-destructive behavior was an attention-seeking mechanism, she says. She received the attention she needed from her 10th grade art teacher, who connected with her. Ms. Thompson enjoyed going to art class, and her teacher's encouragement built up her confidence and refocused her attention on school. The teacher entered a still-life Ms. Thompson painted into a contest, and she won first place. The teacher gave her an ultimatum—if she wanted to continue attending the art class, she would have to attend all of her other classes. She agreed to attend her other classes regularly. The art teacher's efforts to get Ms. Thompson back on track inspired her to consider a career in teaching. She wanted to help other children the way her art teacher helped her. But she decided to go to art school to pursue her interest in art instead.

The art school had a community outreach program through which college students taught art to inner-city children. To help pay for college, Ms. Thompson signed on to teach in the program. The positive experience she had working with the children in the community art program resurrected her notions of becoming a teacher.

The summer after graduating from college, she backpacked through Europe with her future husband. When she returned, she taught at a private elementary school for a year to make sure she was well-suited for teaching before pursuing her master's degree in education. To attain her master's degree, she worked at a nursery school during the day and attended school at night. She worked at the nursery school for four years before accepting a position at an elementary school in New York City. She had limited resources and a classroom of 30 students whose profound needs overwhelmed her. She left at the end of the school year due to professional differences with the principal. (Ms. Thompson's experience in New York is covered in Chapter 1).

As difficult as her experience in New York City was, it didn't tarnish her attitude toward teaching. She didn't consider leaving the teaching profession until she worked in a wealthy suburb in New York as a first grade teacher. When she was hired, the principal told her the job was 90% public relations and 10% teaching. Immediately, she felt disillusioned.

In the weeks that followed, any respect she had for the principal quickly dissipated. The principal did not support the staff, and she was primarily concerned with pleasing the parents. "The parents ruled the school. It was unhealthy," Ms. Thompson says. She was forced to give students higher grades than they deserved or move them into a higher reading group because of demands from the parents. "There was no respect for the teachers," she says.

The principal told her when she was hired that if she wanted to receive tenure, she should not get pregnant. To protect her job, she delayed having children for three years until she was 31. At that time, she had difficulty conceiving and suspects her decision to postpone having children was to blame.

While she was undergoing fertility treatment, she had a student in her class who refused to do his work. After numerous calls home, she finally decided to require the student to do his work in the classroom during recess, even though it meant she had to give up her own lunch time. Her decision upset the student's parents, who requested a conference with the principal. At the conference, the child's father maintained that it was Ms. Thompson's fault the child was not doing his work and questioned her teaching ability and her commitment to her job. Unaware she was undergoing fertility treatment, he said to her, "I wish I could pull out an EPT test and make you pee on the stick because I don't want a pregnant teacher." The remark amused the principal, who started laughing. Ms. Thompson lost her composure and began to cry. The principal told her she had no sense of humor.

After the conference, Ms. Thompson requested to have the student removed from her class because she could not deal with the child's father again. She had never made such a request before, even though she had a lot of difficult students. The principal placed many of the students with behavior issues in Ms. Thompson's class because of her background as a New York City school teacher. Ms. Thompson acknowledges she was adept at classroom management and was fully capable of handling behavior problems. But in this case, the student was not the issue—it was the parent. The principal agreed to Ms. Thompson's request, and the parents were pleased that their child was reassigned. However, three weeks later, they expressed their disappointment with the new teacher and asked to have their son returned to Ms. Thompson's class. She refused to take the student back.

When Ms. Thompson informed the principal she was pregnant, the principal concealed news of the pregnancy from the parents for fear of upsetting them. When Ms. Thompson was 10 minutes late to class on four occasions due to prenatal visits to her doctor, the parents found out from their children and vehemently complained. She made sure to schedule her appointments first thing in the morning, when her students went to a special (such as art or gym), and she arranged for a colleague to supervise them for 10 minutes after the special until she arrived. The reaction from the parents upset her because she had proved herself to be a dedicated teacher—she volunteered on several committees, she and her husband designed T-shirts for a fundraiser, and she maintained a file that was brimming with positive feedback from parents. "I jumped through a lot of hoops," she says. She felt that the principal could have avoided the complaints had she notified the parents about the pregnancy. The parents were unaware she had a legitimate reason for being late.

Ms. Thompson felt disrespected by parents on multiple occasions. One parent incessantly complained to Ms. Thompson that her child was being bullied on the school bus, a situation teachers have little control over. Yet Ms. Thompson attempted to help the child by talking to him and suggesting strategies for dealing with the bully. Then the parent complained that her advice made the child feel that it was his fault he was being bullied.

She had another student who was disturbing the classmates at his table and preventing them from doing their work. She removed him from the situation by giving him a time out—he had to sit at a table by himself for a few minutes. The parents called the principal to complain. Ms. Thompson was upset at the parents' reaction because she had developed a good relationship with them when she taught their older child the year before.

She says the principal was largely to blame for the parents' behavior. The principal created an environment in which parents felt comfortable contacting her to lodge complaints against teachers. The principal made a concerted effort to appease the parents—often at her staff's expense—therefore empowering the parents.

Ms. Thompson enjoys talking about her experience in New York City—she looks back on it with nostalgia—but her experience in the suburbs makes her angry because "it didn't have to be that way." She left after six years at the school to raise her children. Both of her children will attend school full time next year, and she plans to return to teaching. But she will carefully choose the school districts where she applies; she doesn't want to work in a school district that is known for its political atmosphere and focus on pleasing parents at any cost.

"I'm not putting up with crap and nonsense," she says.

Her priorities have changed as well. She is motivated and looking forward to resuming her career, but she's not as focused on job security. If she's not enjoying her job, she will not hesitate to leave her tenure track and move to a new school district.

* * *

Sharon Hill, Elementary School Teacher, New York

Sharon Hill had been teaching fourth and fifth grade in a suburban district in New York for 13 years when she felt it was time to reevaluate her career. She was recently divorced after helping her husband battle a mental illness for years. After the divorce, she moved with her young son into an apartment. She had little money, no furniture and slept on a cot. "But I put on a smile because I knew my responsibilities to the children. I'm known as one of the happiest, most loving people," she says. "I don't have a regular job. I can't come in unhappy. So I faked it all day long."

She felt her school district had become too focused on test results. "I'm a more holistic teacher," she says. "I'm child-centered." She wanted a teaching position in which she could attend to the emotional and psychological well-being of her students, as well as their academic needs.

Ms. Hill decided to pursue a position teaching kindergarten to rejuvenate her enthusiasm for teaching. A position was available in another school in her district, but the administration had already moved a non-tenured colleague of hers into the job. Her colleague, a man who had been teaching for 15 years, felt he did not have the patience to teach a kindergarten class. She agreed it was not a good fit. "If you don't want to be on the floor with blocks, you're going to lose it in two days," she says. "They wanted to put him there so they could push him around; it was degrading." She volunteered to take the kindergarten position so her colleague could remain at the fifth grade level.

Despite her financial situation, Ms. Hill spent between $2,000 and $3,000 to decorate her new classroom and purchase supplies. The district gave her about $130 to spend on supplies for the year.

She asserts that the principal resented her for interfering with the original selection for the open kindergarten position, and retaliated by placing in her class all of the students who had behavior problems or parents who were known to be demanding and difficult.

Ms. Hill has a master's degree in special education, and she quickly identified students who required special services. She requested the students receive the necessary services, but maintains that the principal intentionally slowed down the process. In addition to the students who required intervention, she had a multitude of other issues to deal with. She had a student who was particularly defiant and disrespectful. She had another student who couldn't walk across the room without crying.

While many of the children had behavioral problems, required special education intervention, or were disruptive, two students were reading on a second grade level. Early in the year, the parents of the two readers demanded to know how she was going to cater to the needs of their children. "And they're right," she says, acknowledging that the parents were entitled to advocate for their children, and she was responsible for ensuring the students received the attention they deserved.

Taking cues from business books she read while previously considering a career change, she began to run her classroom like a business. "I considered each child a client and the parents clients," she says. "I got very creative."

She stayed up late at night developing plans for each of the children. She kept pushing the administration until all of the students who required special services received them. She enlisted the help of the reading specialists to create gifted programs for the two advanced readers in her class. As for her student who was particularly obstinate, she treated him like a leader to channel his negative behavior in a positive way and managed to change his attitude.

By the end of the year, all of the students were reading and writing. "The kids loved school, and the parents were happy," she says.

She contends that most of the first grade teachers, who would have her students the following year, stopped speaking to her because she had raised the parents' expectations.

She asserts that teachers are partly to blame if they have adversarial relationships with parents. Many teachers are overqualified—they have master's degrees, doctorates, and extensive experience—and they resent interference from parents. But teachers should make an effort to enlist the help of parents, who usually know their children best, and develop positive partnerships with them to benefit the children.

* * *

Sarah Brown, Middle School Teacher, New York

When Sarah Brown finished graduate school and received her master's degree, she pursued a teaching position at the middle school she attended as a child (see Chapter 2). The incoming sixth grade class the following fall was expected to have 20 more students than the previous year. Although the middle school teachers typically focused on one subject, the position she was offered would require her to teach more than one subject due to the enrollment spike. She was expected to teach one period of sixth grade math, one period of sixth grade English, one period of sixth grade social studies, and one period of eighth grade math strategies every day. She was also expected to teach one period of sixth grade math strategies every other day.

Because the sixth grade strategies class took place every other day, the position was not considered full-time, and she received 90% of the standard full-time salary and benefits.

The administrators told Ms. Brown they discussed her hybrid position with the current English, math and social studies teachers, and they agreed to collaborate with her and support her since she had to prepare for classes in five subjects while most teachers prepared for one. Since her goal was to be a math teacher, she felt well-prepared to teach the math classes; it was the English and social studies classes that concerned her. The social studies teacher she would be working with, Ron Lloyd, was in his second year teaching in the district. Ms. Brown was looking forward to learning the curriculum from him. She intended to use his lesson plans as a foundation for designing her own lessons based on her style and vision. But Ms. Brown soon discovered that Mr. Lloyd was not interested in assisting her.

"This teacher refused to meet with me and share his ideas because it was a waste of his time," she says. "Instead, he suggested I sit in on one of his classes every day, and then after school redesign the lesson based on my own ideas and teach it the following day."

Since Ms. Brown was a new teacher and didn't have any other options, she gave up one of her prep periods every day to sit in on one of his classes and observe the lesson. She spent another period designing activities for her own class the following day.

The English teacher, Jackie Morgan, approached her relationship with Ms. Brown differently from Mr. Lloyd. Ms. Morgan suggested they split the workload in half. Ms. Brown agreed to Ms. Morgan's plan, but soon discovered they had different ideas of what sharing the workload meant. For example, when they were using a book for a unit of study, Ms. Brown thought they should each read the book, develop questions and share them with one another. Ms. Morgan suggested they alternate books—if it was Ms. Brown's turn to design the lessons and activities for the book, Ms. Morgan wouldn't read the book; she would rely on Ms. Brown's answer keys. Ms. Brown realized that to Ms. Morgan, sharing the workload meant cutting her own workload in half.

Ms. Brown's encounters with Mr. Lloyd and Ms. Morgan occurred eight years ago. Neither Mr. Lloyd nor Ms. Morgan received tenure and were forced to leave the school district. Ms. Brown was offered tenure and currently works with a supportive and close-knit team of teachers. But she has faced issues with a few parents over the years. While she feels she has fostered positive relationships with most of the parents, the handful who don't support her efforts on behalf of their children frustrate her. One of her students forged a parent's signature on a progress report. She called the student's mother, who assured her the boy would face consequences at home and asked that he not face disciplinary action at school. When the next round of progress reports were distributed, the student approached Ms. Brown privately and asked if he had to have the progress report signed. She replied, "Yes, please have it signed *by a parent*." Another student overheard the exchange, concluded the student had forged a parent's signature previously, and taunted him about it. The next day, Ms. Brown received a lengthy and angry voice mail message from the student's mother, chastising her for discussing the family's personal business in front of the class. Two weeks later, another teacher called the same student's mother to inform her that her son forged a signature on a progress report. The mother simply sent the teacher an e-mail message stating, "I'll take care of it."

On another occasion, three sixth grade boys were reprimanded for telling highly offensive anti-Semitic and racist jokes. Several months later, one of the boys used Ms. Brown's classroom telephone to call his mother and ordered her in a haughty and belligerent manner to deliver his baseball equipment to him at school. After receiving his baseball equipment, the student threatened to hit another student with the baseball bat. Ms. Brown confiscated the baseball bat, but the student proceeded to chase his intended target around the room until dismissal. Ms. Brown brought up the incident during a team meeting, and the team decided to ban the student from the end-of-year pool party. When the parents were notified by the team leader, they accused Ms. Brown of mistreating their son because she is Jewish and was offended by his anti-Semitic jokes earlier in the year. They unexpectedly appeared at school and demanded a meeting with Ms. Brown, where they pressured her to allow their son to attend the pool party.

"They said I was scarring him for life by not letting him go to the pool party," she says. The principal sided with the parents and asked the sixth grade team to reconsider, but the sixth grade team stood by their decision.

Ms. Brown's colleague, Peggy Scott, recently faced a frustrating experience involving two parents. The seventh grade was scheduled to take a two-night field trip. Seven students chose not to go on the trip. Ms. Scott, who was not attending the trip, volunteered to plan three days of lessons for the students who would remain in school. She spent weeks preparing the lessons—collaborating with the other teachers, creating activities and designing a schedule for the students since no seventh grade classes would be in session. She made sure the three days would be filled with meaningful educational activities that paralleled the events on the field trip.

The seven students and their parents received the schedules a few days in advance. The afternoon before the first day of the trip, two parents came into school to complain about the planned schedule. Ms. Scott defended the validity of the plans. One mother insisted that the three days at school should mirror the educational activities taking place on the trip. Ms. Scott explained how her lesson plans accomplished that goal. Then the mother went on to say that her son chose not to go on the trip because he had been to a similar place and did not enjoy himself. Now Ms. Scott was confused about why the mother insisted that the lesson plans reflect the activities on the trip if her son was not interested in them.

Dissatisfied with Ms. Scott's explanation, the parents approached the principal, who also defended the quality of the lesson plans. The next day—the first day of the field trip—one of the students called his mother to complain he was displeased with his schedule. In particular, he did not want to go to one of the teachers he was assigned, and preferred another teacher. His mother told him to go to the office. One of the secretaries called Ms. Scott to ask her if the student could switch to a different class. She objected because the teacher already planned a lesson incorporating the student and the other teacher did not. The secretary then told Ms. Scott she already sent the student to the other teacher. Although the student's request was accommodated, he complained to his mother when he arrived home that he did not have a pleasant day. This time, the mother visited the office of the superintendent, who was too busy to see her. But the superintendent received a message from the mother, which prompted her to call Ms. Scott, the principal and the vice principal to her office to discuss the matter. The superintendent agreed with Ms. Scott and the principal, but asked them to change the schedules to appease the parent anyway.

That night, the principal called another teacher and asked her to redesign the lesson plan for the following morning. The teacher was uncomfortable defying the principal, so she spent the entire evening creating the lesson plan. Ms. Scott told the principal that several teachers and student mentors were involved in her lesson plans, and urged her to notify them of the changes. But the principal neglected to take Ms. Scott's suggestion. The following day, chaos surrounded the students who didn't go on the field trip. The student mentors who were supposed to be working with them became nervous when they failed to show up at the times designated on Ms. Scott's schedule. Teachers who agreed to incorporate the seven students into their lessons extemporaneously changed their lessons when the students did not appear. Other teachers who were not expecting the seven students also had to improvise when the students showed up in their classrooms. One of the teachers was particularly displeased because she happened to be undergoing an evaluation by the principal that day.

Ms. Brown says the students at her school have also impugned the reputations of teachers. One of her colleagues, Tom Fuller, a technology teacher, has a middle school class followed by a high school class. A few minutes before the middle school period ended one day, a boy in the class starting playing with a metal contraption Mr. Fuller prepared for a demonstration for his high school students the following period. By tinkering with the pieces, the student was effectively destroying the demonstration. The student had misbehaved in the class on a number of previous occasions, and nothing Mr. Fuller said seemed to work. He asked the boy to stop touching the device three times. The student proceeded to dismantle the contraption. Mr. Fuller took a piece out of the student's hands and tapped him on the head with it. The student was wearing a hard hat because he had been working on the machines in the room. Mr. Fuller then ripped up the student's technology handout to demonstrate that destroying property belonging to other people is unacceptable.

As Mr. Fuller walked away, he overheard a group of boys warning the student that Mr. Fuller was going to report him and he would likely be barred from playing in the football game that afternoon. The students suggested to their friend that he report his version of the incident to the principal first.

Mr. Fuller had three minutes to conceive of a new lesson for his next class since his demonstration was destroyed. While he was busy preparing for the class, the group of boys visited the main office and told the assistant principal that he hit the student hard on the head, angrily shredded his paper, and now they were afraid to be in the class with him and refused to return. The assistant principal told Mr. Fuller what the boys said, and he then gave his version of what happened. He also called the student's parents to explain. The boy's father said he didn't think it was right that Mr. Fuller tore the paper, but offered to pay for the damages to Mr. Fuller's demonstration.

The incident was reminiscent of a similar episode Mr. Fuller was involved in about a month after the school district hired him. One of

Mr. Fuller's students sneaked into a closet in his classroom and hid there, causing him to frantically search for the student. When he discovered the student was in the closet, he reported the incident to the principal's office. To avoid disciplinary action, the student claimed to his parents that Mr. Fuller locked him in the closet. The parents complained to the superintendent, and the superintendent instructed the assistant principal to fire Mr. Fuller immediately. When Mr. Fuller was informed of this decision, he asked for an opportunity to defend himself. The principal, who supported Mr. Fuller, called the parents in for a conference. The father, who was aware that Mr. Fuller had previously taught in New York City, condescendingly informed him that locking children in closets might be acceptable at his former school, but it was not condoned in their school district. After Mr. Fuller explained that the student had locked himself in the closet, the principal asked the other students in the class what happened. They all corroborated Mr. Fuller's version of the incident, and he was allowed to keep his job.

* * *

Politics and the Public School

Internal political struggles aside, public school systems are, by nature, part of the broader political landscape because they are supervised and funded by state and federal agencies. Many teachers feel enormous pressure to ensure their students perform well on standardized state tests, particularly since enactment of the No Child Left Behind Act.

The goal of the No Child Left Behind Act of 2001 (NCLB Act) is to ensure that all students are meeting academic standards and to hold school districts accountable for student progress. The NCLB Act requires states to test students in reading and math every year in grades three to eight and at least once in high school. School districts are expected to make adequate yearly progress (AYP) toward state reading and math goals. Schools and districts that fail to achieve AYP are, over time, subjected to corrective actions. School districts are required to publish annual report cards to inform parents and the community of student achievement levels on state assessments.

Nicole Evans, who has taught third and fourth grade (looped classes) in Connecticut for the past six years, says the most frustrating aspect of her job is the pressure to make sure students achieve success on state tests due to the NCLB Act. Regardless of the standardized tests, teachers aim to challenge and motivate their students to achieve academic success every day. But other factors stand in the way of attaining this goal. Parents have asked Ms. Evans to excuse their children from homework assignments because of hockey tournaments, family trips, pageants, or other extracurricular activities and events. Students do not take responsibility for completing their assignments and face no consequences. Ms. Evans is not permitted to take recess time away when students fail to complete their work. She is concerned that children are getting the message that after-school activities take precedence over school work. "When the parents get the test scores and they are low, they come running to us wondering what happened, asking us what we did wrong, what we didn't teach their child in order to pass the test," she says.

Ruth Mitchell, who has been an educator in New York City for 28 years, contends that schools are so focused on test scores due to the NCLB Act that they are stifling teachers' creativity. "The power has been taken from teachers," she says. "Everything is a script now." She is currently a middle school speech pathologist, but she has been an elementary school teacher, a special education teacher and a teacher trainer. As a trainer, she encouraged teachers to spend an extra five minutes to seize "a teachable moment." But she claims this flexibility is no longer possible because the teacher's time is so structured.

Sarah Brown, a middle school math teacher in a New York suburb, says teachers who claim the focus on testing squelches creativity are making excuses. The tests reflect the curriculum the state provides; as long as a teacher follows the curriculum, students will be prepared for the tests. Teachers can teach the curriculum any way they want, and they can be as innovative as they choose to be. She acknowledges that the curriculum is quite specific, and there is a lot of material to get through in a limited amount of time. And there are always interruptions that throw off the schedule, such as snow days, assemblies and absenteeism. Thus teachers face a lot of pressure to get through the subject matter by the time the test rolls around.

The most stressful aspect of test preparation is that teachers must rely on each student's sense of responsibility and level of motivation, Ms. Brown says. In other occupations, employees who face deadline pressure are relying on cooperation from other adults. They may be incompetent, but at least they understand that their jobs and livelihoods are at stake. Some children are not mature or motivated enough to understand that they have a vested interest in performing well in school. And if undisciplined students don't study for exams or do their homework, and they don't perform adequately on the tests, it reflects poorly on the teacher.

Ms. Brown admits she can prepare and present a truly innovative, exciting lesson only once every other week because of limited preparation time during the school day and limited class time. But she says her teaching style keeps the students engaged every lesson. She has a fun personality and the students enjoy her sense of humor. She prepares lessons and grades papers during free periods and lunch periods to avoid staying late and working at home.

Susan Johnson, a retired teacher from Tennessee, contends that schools and teachers should not be penalized for poor test scores. Sometimes circumstances arise that prevent a child from performing well on a test on a particular day. For instance, a child might have had a difficult experience at home the night before. "People want education to function like industry; we're working with human beings," she says. She believes teachers should have more input into the educational system.

Ms. Johnson says dealing with the state education department bureaucracy can be frustrating for teachers. When one of her students vomited on her Tennessee math assessment test one year, the test was discarded. The state education department refused to supply the school with the processed test scores because of the missing test, although the school repeatedly provided an explanation. The next year, another student vomited on the test. Ms. Johnson sent the vomit-covered test to the education department in a Ziploc bag.

[Editor's Note: An official at the Tennessee Department of Education says the incident Ms. Johnson described probably occurred prior to the enactment of the No Child Left Behind Act, before the urgency to receive test scores existed. She says a new testing system has been put in place since then. While she is unfamiliar with this particular incident, she notes that the department follows strict security measures to ensure a security breach did not occur before processing test scores. The school district is responsible for investigating the circumstances surrounding an irregularity, such as a missing test, and reporting its findings to the Department of Education.]

Chapter Five

Occupational Hazards

"You tell yourself it's your job and to leave your job at school, and you try to set clear limits. But there are things that creep into your mind and stay there."

Erica Stevens, High School Teacher, California

Children in Crisis

Erica Stevens, High School Teacher, California

Erica Stevens joined Teach For America after she graduated from college. She was assigned to a high school in Los Angeles as an English teacher. The program lasted for two years, but she stayed for another four. The job was stressful because the support system was limited. "I definitely had the sense that I was absolutely the last and only line of defense," she says. She was responsible for "anything and everything at any given moment." If something broke in her room, she had to fix it; if a student appeared to be suicidal, she had to handle it.

Because she taught ninth through 12th grade, she had a girl in her class for the second year in a row. The girl, a junior, was a solid B student the previous year; now she was receiving Ds and Fs. "Her grades took a nosedive," Ms. Stevens says.

She pulled the student outside into the hall one day and asked her why her grades were slipping. The girl was initially reluctant to discuss the reason her grades were suffering. She eventually confided to Ms. Stevens that her brother-in-law was sexually molesting her, and she finally told her family about it when he started to abuse her five-year-old sister. After the student's revelation to her family, her older sister left her husband and moved back to her family's house. But the sister and the rest of the family blamed her for her brother-in-law's behavior, asserting that she invited it. The sister obtained a restraining order against her husband, but he showed up at the house several nights a week and stood beneath the window. The girl was crying in the hallway while she recounted the story.

It's not unusual for a conversation about school performance to lead to a discussion topic that teachers are not equipped to handle.

"A lot of times when this happens, all you can do is listen," Ms. Stevens says, adding that she doesn't have the resources or training to help students in emotional distress. "It's really awful. All you can say is, 'That sounds hard to deal with.'"

Still, she tried to offer support to the student. The girl sometimes stayed after school and talked to her. When the school attempted to transfer the student to a school closer to her home because of her poor attendance record, Ms. Stevens helped her avoid the move. She brought the student to the assistant principal's office to explain her situation. When the student was unable to speak, Ms. Stevens explained the situation for her.

Despite her lack of training in counseling teenagers who are in crisis, Ms. Stevens does what she can to help. When a ninth grade student confided to Ms. Stevens that she was raped, Ms. Stevens helped her report the incident to the police.

To protect herself from becoming emotionally drained by the problems her students bring to her, Ms. Stevens adopts a different persona as a teacher. "When you're there at school, you're another person; you're not fully yourself," she says. She likens the transformation to turning off a switch inside of her. She says she needs to be strong and avoid becoming upset in order to help her students.

But it's not always easy to separate herself from every situation. "You tell yourself it's your job and to leave your job at school, and you try to set clear limits," she says. "But there are things that creep into your mind and stay there."

Despite her efforts to remain personally detached from her students, she admits she can't avoid feeling frustrated and helpless when her efforts to help a student succeed academically prove futile. Ms. Stevens taught a student who she believed was dyslexic. The student was a bright girl who exhibited all of the classic signs of the learning disability. Ms. Stevens wanted to have the girl tested for dyslexia so she could qualify for special education services. She met with the girl's father, who was not fluent in English. Ms. Stevens explained that his daughter was not making as much progress as she could be, but tests were available to determine how the school could help her. He agreed to the tests. When the girl's older sister found out, she became upset because she felt there was a stigma associated with special education services. The sister claimed Ms. Stevens tricked her father into agreeing to the tests. "I had an administrator tell me I was a racist," Ms. Stevens says. The student did not receive the services.

She also feels dejected when her efforts to help students overcome their personal struggles fail. "Too many kids are too far down the path to destruction," she says. Three weeks into the year, the school reorganized class schedules and she got a whole new group of students. One of her new students, apparently displeased by the changes, muttered, "Fuck this," when he walked into the class. She brought him into the hallway and made it clear that she would not tolerate his language. But her difficulties with the student escalated. The boy refused to do any work or participate in class.

The class was discussing a vignette in the book *The House on Mango Street* in which the main character describes the hair of members of her family. When she describes her own hair, she says it's messy and unkempt. Ms. Stevens asked the class what the passage meant and they struggled to come up with an answer. One student ventured: she doesn't worry about her appearance. But that wasn't quite what Ms. Stevens was looking for. Meanwhile, the student who Ms. Stevens was having problems with all year began making disruptive noises during the discussion. She asked him if he would care to comment on the book. He declined. She pressed him. Finally, he said the character's hair reflects her personality; her hair is unruly and she can't be restrained by societal forces. Realizing from his perceptive analysis of the book that the student was gifted, Ms. Stevens looked at him and said, "You can say fuck in my class any time you want."

"He laughed. It broke the ice," she says. Whenever he got into trouble for fighting, disrupting another class or swearing, Ms. Stevens went to the dean's office and defended the student. She tried to talk to him, encourage him and motivate him to straighten out. Yet he continued to fail in school and refused to leave the gang he joined. After six years at the school—four more than she had committed to as part of Teach For America—she left because she was exhausted and she needed a change. The year after she left, she found out the student was shot in the head and killed. (Ms. Stevens' experience at her next job in Massachusetts is covered in Chapter 3.)

* * *

When teachers enter their classrooms in the beginning of the school year, they know their responsibilities will extend beyond educating the students on their rosters. They will not only be dealing with each student's academic abilities, but they will also be facing any emotional, social or behavioral issues that arise during the year. Because such issues may affect a student's classroom behavior and academic performance, teachers must address them. Furthermore, teachers get to know their students and gain insight into their lives through their writing, artwork, comments during class discussions, and social interactions. Thus a teacher will often uncover a personal problem a student is concealing and will feel compelled to help the student in some way. Sometimes, a student will confide a problem to his or her teacher because the teacher is the only trusted adult the student knows. In short, teachers do not view their students only as students; they view them as human beings. They address the whole child, taking into account the child's personality and background.

The responsibility of helping a student who is facing a personal problem, such as a mental health issue or a life crisis, can be emotionally draining and overwhelming for a teacher. Teachers also face the pressure of determining how much help they should provide. They feel torn between their instinct to help a student in trouble and their sense of professionalism, which prevents them from getting too involved.

Middle school and high school teachers cope with a host of problems affecting teenagers (see sidebar).

Mental Health Issues Affecting Teenagers

- ◆ Alcohol and Drug Abuse
- ◆ Anorexia Nervosa
- ◆ Anxiety
- ◆ Attention Deficit Hyperactivity Disorder (ADHD)
- ◆ Bipolar Disorder (Manic-Depression)
- ◆ Bulimia Nervosa (Bulimia)
- ◆ Conduct Disorder
- ◆ Depression
- ◆ Learning Disorders
- ◆ Obsessive-Compulsive Disorder (OCD)
- ◆ Physical Abuse
- ◆ Post-Traumatic Stress Disorder (PTSD)
- ◆ Psychosis
- ◆ Schizophrenia
- ◆ Sexual Abuse
- ◆ Suicide
- ◆ Tourette's Syndrome

Source: American Academy of Child & Adolescent Psychiatry.

All 50 states and Washington, D.C. have laws requiring certain professionals, including teachers, to report suspected incidences of abuse and neglect to a child protective services agency. About 3.3 million reports of the suspected maltreatment of about 6 million children were made to child protective services agencies in 2005, according to the Administration for Children & Families. More than half of the reports were made by professionals including educators, police officers, lawyers and social services staff. The rest were made by friends, relatives and neighbors. An estimated 899,000 children were determined to be victims of neglect, physical abuse, sexual abuse or emotional maltreatment. When reporting cases of suspected abuse or neglect, teachers are sometimes afraid of retaliation from the child's family. They also feel frustrated and helpless when the agency receiving the report is slow to respond.

* * *

Samantha Parker, High School Teacher, New Jersey

Samantha Parker started teaching the September after she graduated from college in 2002. She attended graduate school to attain her degree in educational leadership in 2003, and graduated in 2005. She teaches high school mathematics for grades nine through 12 in New Jersey, and she is currently in her second year as supervisor of the mathematics department.

"I became a teacher because I wanted to make positive changes in the lives of young people," she says. "I wanted to be a role model for young students and show them through my teaching and example that dedication and passion in life will help them to accomplish great things." She considers herself a lifelong learner and wanted to be involved in academia.

She served as an advisor to a student club in which students discuss and address social issues. At one meeting, students were talking about self-esteem issues, and a few of the students disclosed that they engaged in cutting—they intentionally inflicted cuts on themselves to relieve their emotional pain and frustrations.

Suddenly overcome with a deep sense of responsibility for these students, she faced an internal conflict about what she should do with the information she had just learned about them. She did not want to cross the line between professionalism and friendship, nor did she want to betray her students' trust by calling their parents. But she felt compelled to protect them in some way. "I can't forget the feeling I had, not knowing whether these students were safe that night," she says.

She trains five students to run another youth program during the summer. Because she has a good relationship with the students in the program, she asked them to visit the three students she was worried about that night and make sure they were okay.

Maintaining professional boundaries is Ms. Parker's biggest

challenge as a teacher. She enjoys working with her students, and she wants to be able to help them with their problems, but she struggles with the question of how deeply she should get involved. "If a student knows you're willing to listen, you won't believe the things they'll tell you. I didn't expect that," she says.

Over the years, she has learned to separate herself from her job when she goes home at the end of the day. "When I first started, I felt the world on my shoulders," she says. Now she tries to leave her "baggage" in her classroom.

But she doesn't shed her identity as a teacher when she leaves the classroom. Her job is always on her mind. When she's shopping, she'll think about how she can apply the experience to a lesson. When she's on vacation, she'll pick up an education magazine. "I'm a teacher," she says. "It's who I am." She's proud of the contribution she's making. "I think education is vital to our society," she says. She plans to pursue her doctorate to further her own education.

* * *

Karen Harris, High School Teacher, New York

Karen Harris, a teacher at a private high school for girls in New York City, had an uneasy feeling about the behavior of one of her students. The girl's parents were divorced, and she was estranged from her father, who had remarried. She lived with her mother, who had a boyfriend.

The student was attractive, but made an effort to conceal it. She often made negative comments about boys. Ms. Harris sensed the student was struggling with a serious issue in her personal life. The girl felt comfortable with Ms. Harris and spent time talking to her and e-mailing her. She told Ms. Harris she didn't like to go home when her mother's boyfriend was there, but she wouldn't explain why.

Ms. Harris started to suspect the student was being molested by her mother's boyfriend, and she became overwhelmed with concern. Finally, she directly asked the student what was happening when her mother's boyfriend was at home. But the girl became defensive and shut down.

The student became physically ill and frequently vomited at school. Ms. Harris found out the student's mother had invited her boyfriend to move into their home.

"I knew I had to move on this," she says, but she didn't have any proof. She asked the student again what was going on. This time, the girl began to open up to Ms. Harris. She said her mother's boyfriend made inappropriate comments, remarking that the girl should wear tighter shirts and shorter shorts. She said he rubbed up against her. She finally revealed that he was sexually abusing her. She then asked Ms. Harris not to disclose her secret to anyone. But Ms. Harris felt she had to protect the student. She reported the abuse, as she was obligated by law to do.

"She lashed out at me. She was mad that I betrayed her," Ms. Harris says. "She moved out of my class. But I did what I needed to do, even if she never spoke to me again." Although she knew she did the right thing, she was consumed with guilt because of the student's reaction. "It did eat me up inside."

The student graduated at the end of that year. About a year and a half later, the girl returned to the school to thank Ms. Harris for helping her. Ms. Harris continues to keep in touch with her.

* * *

Patricia Thomas, Elementary School Teacher, New York

Patricia Thomas says her first grade class in New York City was sweet, compliant and eager to please her. But one of the boys "was the wildest child I had ever seen." When the class was lined up, he would dash out and run along the side of the line, slamming the children behind their knees so they would fall like dominoes. He flew around the classroom, sweeping everything from the desks. The other children would sit at their desks dutifully writing when all of a sudden their pencils and paper would go flying. He was fast, and Ms. Thomas could not catch him. He would dart, run and crawl to escape her. She spent the day trying to protect the other children, who were terrified of him. She doesn't recall ever hearing the child speak.

Ms. Thomas, a new teacher, had three young children of her own, a husband with a terminal illness, and no money. She knew she had to find a way to deal with the situation in her classroom because she needed her job. She tried referring the child for special education services, but the process was slow. She tried calling the child's mother, who said she called 911 to control her son at home. That was not an option for Ms. Thomas. She tried calming him down with soft words, candy, threats—but nothing worked.

She was reluctant to take the student on a class trip to the Statue of Liberty, but the principal did not want to keep him in the building. She asked the boy's mother to come along on the trip because she was afraid he would run off, and she had to take care of the other children. The mother agreed to accompany the class on the trip.

During the trip, the class was eating lunch in the park. The benches where the children sat had wooden slats for seats and wooden slats for backs. When the boy started to get up, Ms. Thomas watched his mother to see how she would get him to sit still. "She took the side of her arm and wailed this tiny child across his gut so hard that it sent him bent in half through the space between the slats and onto the ground behind the bench," Ms. Thomas says. "He was still and obviously in shock. I turned away, ready to throw up."

* * *

Laura Taylor, Elementary School Teacher, New York

Laura Taylor taught elementary school in an urban district in New York State. She felt her students enjoyed coming to school because she gave them positive reinforcement, cared about them, and provided an environment that was often more secure and nurturing than their homes.

"I loved these kids. I felt I was making such a difference," she says. She spent half of her salary on supplies. She stayed at the school for five years until she had a baby and decided to stop working.

On the first day of school in her first year, the main office contacted Ms. Taylor on the intercom and asked if a particular student in her first grade class was present. The girl was not. The next day, the same thing happened. After a few days, the girl finally showed up. She was placed in first grade for the third year in a row because she had missed so many days of school the first two times that she could not move on to second grade. She was eight years old now, but she looked like she could be in first grade because she was so small and frail. She appeared to be malnourished. She looked like she hadn't bathed or washed her hair in a while and wore dirty clothing. She had no academic skills; she couldn't read or write and she barely spoke. The child evoked Ms. Taylor's maternal instinct. "She was so cute I wanted to take her home," she says.

Ms. Taylor spoke to the school principal regarding her concerns about the girl. The principal was well aware of the situation, having had the student in first grade for two years prior. She said the child's mother was neglectful and didn't often send her to school, and she advised Ms. Taylor to do the best she could to deal with the situation.

Ms. Taylor tried contacting the child's mother, but was unable to reach her. After the child missed more than 100 days of school, Ms. Taylor informed the principal she was going to notify the social services agency, as she was legally bound to do. The principal agreed, but indicated she would not get involved. Ms. Taylor remembers seeing a number of news stories that year about children being found dead in dumpsters and was always astonished that something like that could happen. "Now I believed it after seeing this child," she says.

Ms. Taylor told the social services agent that the child was not showing up regularly for school, as the law required. The girl would not appear for three weeks at a time, then she would suddenly show up, usually late. The social services agency was already familiar with the child and had a file on her. She made two follow-up calls to press the agency to intervene.

Shortly after, she received a phone call from the child's mother. The woman was irate, screaming into the phone, "You fucking bitch, you better stop calling social services on me. Mind your own fucking business." Ms. Taylor tried to explain to the child's mother that she was concerned because her daughter's skills were so far below the level where they should be. But the woman was furious and irrational.

Ms. Taylor decided she was finished calling social services. She was a single woman, living alone near the school, and she was afraid the child's mother would harm her in some way if she pursued the matter.

One day the girl came to school looking lethargic. At recess, she passed out cold on the playground. She was in such a deep sleep that the aides could not rouse her. They brought her to the nurse. At one point, the girl said her mother had given her medicine. Ms. Taylor felt she had no choice but to call social services again. She told the agent the girl was out cold in the nurse's office and they should send someone to the school right away. The agent said nobody was available to come to the school, and if she was concerned she should take the child to the emergency room. The child stayed in the nurse's office until the end of the day, then she was put on the bus and sent home.

The following year, the child's mother transferred her to a different school.

* * *

Carol Wright, Elementary School Teacher, New York

Carol Wright taught fourth grade at a Catholic school in New York City (see Chapter 4). Although she had 35 students in her class, including 10 with special needs, one of the boys stood out. He routinely built walls around his desk with his books or folders, claiming he had to protect himself. Ms. Wright asked the boy what he needed to protect himself from, but he didn't respond.

Ms. Wright relayed her concerns to the principal, but she didn't provide any guidance. At dismissal time one afternoon, the boy crawled into a ball on the floor and began screaming and crying. He wailed that his father was picking him up from school and he was afraid. She called the office, but the principal wasn't in. Someone else from the office staff came to her classroom because the boy refused to leave. Eventually, he left with his father. She immediately called social services. She spoke with an official at the agency at length, answering questions about the student.

Social services agents visited the boy's house that day, and his father was ultimately arrested for child abuse. Shortly after, the boy's mother came to the school with her son to thank Ms. Wright. The boy hugged her.

She says she didn't consider the possibility of retaliation because she was leaving the school at the end of the year and she had an unlisted phone number. "I always did that purposely as a teacher because it's frightening," she says.

* * *

Confronting Poverty

About 12.8 million children in America, or 17.4%, are living in poverty, according to the U.S. Census Bureau. Observing the adverse affects of poverty on the children in their classes can be emotionally difficult for teachers. Teachers will sometimes purchase food, clothing and supplies for their students. Taking on the responsibility of providing such essentials for up to 30 students can be physically and mentally draining.

* * *

Abby Butler, Elementary School Teacher, California

Abby Butler began teaching after graduating from college. She has been teaching elementary school in California for four years. She taught kindergarten for one year in an urban school district, and has taught first grade for the past three years in a rural farm community.

Many of the children in Ms. Butler's class her first year came from families that were struggling financially; some were homeless. "So many kids have asked to live with me," she says. She tried to find ways to help. She went to Target and purchased an entire wardrobe for one of the girls in her class. Concerned about offending the child's parents, she asked them if she could give the girl the clothing. She told them that if they didn't want the clothes, it was okay; she could take them back. But the parents were grateful and accepted the clothing.

If a child didn't come to school for an extended period of time, she became concerned. Sometimes she would try to call the child's home, only to discover the telephone had been disconnected. But she tried to maintain a positive attitude. "I could only hope for the best," she says. "If the child came back, I was overjoyed."

Teachers and administrators paid for families to stay in hotels, cooked them meals and gave them money. While she helped her students financially, she tried to distance herself emotionally. She didn't give out personal information, including her cell phone number. But she still found herself getting attached to the children in her class. She is still in contact with some of the families she grew close to her first year. She recently attended a birthday party for one of her former students.

Ms. Butler goes to bed at night thinking about the welfare of the children in her class, as well as her lesson plans for the following day. She keeps Post-It notepads at her bedside so she can write notes to herself when ideas enter her mind late at night.

The biggest problem she encountered her first year was the fighting among the children in her class. One girl in her class was particularly difficult. She was bigger than the other children and quite intelligent. She could have been in first grade. While Ms. Butler says she wouldn't describe the child as a bully, the girl had an attitude akin to that of a bully and exhibited tendencies toward aggressive behavior.

The child was physically hostile toward Ms. Butler as well, and often bit her and pulled her hair.

Ms. Butler tried everything she could think of to help the child change her behavior. She spoke with the child's mother daily, sent the child to the office, and scoured her college textbooks for ideas, but nothing she tried was effective. "She drove me nuts. I didn't know what to do with her," she says.

She often called the school's security guard to remove the girl from the classroom and walk her around the building to calm her down. She often asked the principal to come into the classroom to talk to the child. She tried to give the girl incentives to behave. She assigned her more challenging work than the rest of the class to ensure she was adequately stimulated. At the same time, Ms. Butler realized she had 19 other children in her class who needed her attention. "I couldn't focus all of my energy on her," she says. "I could only do so much."

Ironically, the child developed a fondness for Ms. Butler. She looked forward to coming to school and hugged Ms. Butler when she saw her in the morning. But the child still could not control her aggression.

Eventually, Ms. Butler resigned herself to the fact that the child's behavior was not going to improve, and she would have to find a way to live with it the entire year. "I woke up every day and figured she's going to be doing something and I have to deal with it," she says.

Ms. Butler spoke to her own mother—a speech pathologist who has extensive experience working with children—on a daily basis. Her mother offered her advice about dealing with the child, and gave her emotional support. It was helpful for her to have someone to talk to about the problem. If she didn't express her frustration to her mother every day, "I would have gone crazy," she says.

She tried to remain focused on her primary responsibility. The most important thing to her, as a first-year teacher, was that the child met her academic goals despite her behavior.

At the end of the year, the child's parents gave Ms. Butler a present—a large, framed picture of the girl. She considered the gift a token of their appreciation and figured she must have had a positive impact on the family, even though she didn't perceive any notable improvement in the child's behavior. When she went back to the school to visit the year after she left, she discovered the child was behaving the same way in first grade.

Ms. Butler was prepared for a difficult year when she started teaching because she knew the first year is always the toughest. She heard that teachers know if they can make it in the profession within that first year. She got through it because her education prepared her well for the experience, she says. She also benefited from the support she received from her students' parents and from her principal.

Despite the behavior problems she has to deal with, she enjoys her job. "The kids keep me going," she says. "And they say such cute things and make me laugh."

Aside from dealing with challenging behavior problems, she says teachers face considerable pressure from standardized testing. If children do not perform adequately on standardized tests, "the teachers are the scapegoats," she says. Teachers get blamed for low test scores despite the extenuating circumstances that prevent children from performing well, such as difficult home lives, she says.

Teachers are also dissatisfied with their salaries, which they deem unacceptable given their workloads, she says. "We feel most frustrated because of the salaries and benefits. We put in so many hours," she says. "It's sad that we get paid so little for what we do." Ms. Butler's school is in session from 8 a.m. to 3:30 p.m. But she arrives by 7:15 or 7:30 a.m. and leaves at 4 p.m. "on a good day." She is often at school until 5 or 6 p.m. She also spends between two and two-and-a-half hours at home grading papers. She spends hours on the weekends planning her lessons for the week. She knew teachers didn't earn high incomes—she didn't enter the profession for the salary—but she feels teachers deserve more credit for the work they do. It means a lot to her when parents thank her for making a difference in their child's life.

To deal with the stress of her job, Ms. Butler tries to keep active and busy when away from school. She exercises and goes out with friends. She has also learned that a teacher's two best friends should be the school secretary, who knows everything that goes on in the school and everything about the kids and their families, and the security guard (or custodian if the school doesn't have a security guard).

She says statistics show that if a teacher can make it through the first five years, he or she can make it long-term. She's in her fourth year, and she thinks she's "doing okay." But she has a lot of friends from graduate school who have already quit or have obtained a new certification so they don't have to be classroom teachers. Some of her friends are pursuing jobs in related fields. She says she may be ready to change grade levels after teaching first grade for three years, but she remains committed to teaching.

Ms. Butler was in her classroom during a recent school vacation to fill out paperwork for a parent who was having her child evaluated for a psychological disorder. "I promised her I would do it over the vacation," she says.

* * *

Donna King, Elementary School Teacher, New York

Donna King taught in a New York City elementary school for about six years before taking maternity leave when her first child was born. She returned on a part-time basis for a while before moving to the suburbs and obtaining a job in a school district closer to her new home. After taking a maternity leave when her second child was born, she returned to New York City as a substitute teacher one day a week.

Some of the children in Ms. King's classes in New York City wore the same clothing every day, or wore clothing that was too small for them. She purchased supplies, such as crayons and notebooks, for the students who did not bring their own supplies. Teachers and administrators at the school often went grocery shopping for families or brought in clothing for the children.

The mother of one of Ms. King's students said her daughter couldn't go on a class field trip because she didn't have the money to pay for it at the moment. Ms. King didn't want the child to miss out on the trip, so she paid for it. The mother paid her back soon after the trip.

In her first couple of years at the school, Ms. King brought five of her students each summer to her mother's house to use the swimming pool. She stopped because she felt it was unfair to the other children.

While she did what she could for her students, some of them had troubles in their family lives that extended beyond her abilities to help. One day during morning message, which focuses on class news, a boy in her second grade class reported that his father lifted up the floorboard in one of the rooms of their home because that's where he hides his drugs. Ms. King told the guidance counselor, but the school never addressed the student's comment.

During her lunch period one year when she was teaching first grade, Ms. King stepped into the hallway and noticed the mother of one of her students approaching her classroom. Another teacher stood behind the woman, shaking her head, motioning with her hands, and mouthing, "No," ostensibly to warn Ms. King about the woman. She recalls that the woman's daughter was smart, but she was absent from school a lot because she helped care for her three younger siblings. When the woman reached Ms. King's classroom, she asked Ms. King for money. She said she needed to buy food for her children. Ms. King said she didn't have any money with her that day. Her colleagues later told her that they believed the woman wanted the money for drugs, not food. The assistant principal once offered to buy the woman groceries, but she refused; she just wanted money.

Meanwhile, Ms. King found the limited resources in her school district challenging. In her third year, she was given a first grade class in a new school. When she arrived to set up her classroom, she found the room lacked most of the furniture she needed. The room had a few student desks and a file cabinet, which was stuck to the middle of the floor. She had to ask her husband to come in to help her move it. She roamed around the school building scrounging for furniture. By the time school started, she still didn't have enough desks and some of the students had to share a table. Classes were supposed to have 28 students, but she had 31. She didn't have enough books to go around so she made copies at her own expense.

She was most frustrated by the lack of parking for teachers in New York City. The school where she worked has about 10 designated faculty spots, but people living in the neighborhood often obtain parking permits from their friends at other schools and occupy the faculty spots. Teachers must follow the "alternate side of the street parking" rules posted on street signs. If they are parked on the side scheduled to be cleaned, they must move their cars at 11:30 a.m. and double park on the opposite side of the street or they will receive a hefty fine. They have to find co-workers to watch their classes so they can leave the building. At 11:30 a.m., a mass exodus from the school takes place as the teachers file out to move their cars. After they move their cars, they and must go back to move their cars again at 1 p.m. after the street cleaner comes through or they will receive even larger tickets. "It's so stressful," she says. While in the middle of teaching she would have to remember to move her car twice during the day. "It's one of the most annoying things you can ever experience." The parking situation is one of the reasons "people are desperate to leave" their jobs, she says. Teachers' cars are often vandalized.

She says people who want to change careers to become teachers don't realize the job primarily involves disciplining children and dealing with problems all day. She taught an after-school program with a colleague, Mary Williams. At the end of the day, one of the girls aggressively pushed another girl and caused her to cry. When the mother of the girl who pushed her classmate arrived to pick up her daughter, Ms. Williams explained what happened. She suggested they bring the two girls together to talk because the other child was quite upset. The mother took offense to this recommendation. She aggressively shouted directly into Ms. Williams' face that her daughter did nothing wrong. When the other student's father arrived to pick up his daughter and found out what was happening, he began yelling at his daughter that she should not take such abuse and she should punch her attacker. Recognizing the volatility of the scene that had erupted, Ms. King called for the assistant principal because the security guard was not in that day. The assistant principal did not come to assist them.

In the past 10 years, student behavior has deteriorated and her job has become more difficult, Ms. King says. Despite the challenges, she continued to work in the New York City school system all those years because "I had to get paid," she says. She considered leaving teaching to pursue a new career, but then learned of an opening for a full-time reading specialist in a suburban school district near her home. She decided to apply and was offered the job. She has been working in her new school district for about six months and thoroughly enjoys her job. She has a shorter commute, no parking problems, no discipline issues and a wealth of parental support.

* * *

Violence in Schools

Schools aim to provide students and teachers with a safe environment that is conducive to learning. However, incidents of crime and violence do occur, albeit infrequently at most schools. The issue that has received the most attention in recent years is bullying. Cyberbullying—in which a student or group of students use cell phones or the Internet to threaten or verbally abuse a classmate—is a growing concern. When students harass their classmates—whether physically or verbally—teachers are often forced to get involved. Meting out discipline consumes valuable teaching and preparation time. Students who are bullies often engage in other antisocial behaviors, and many teachers find it challenging to get through to them. In addition, teachers have to address the emotional problems that victims may develop, such as low self-esteem, depression and anxiety.

Teachers may also be victims of school violence themselves. In a government survey, 7% of teachers reported they were threatened with injury by a student from their school in the 2003-04 school year, according to *Indicators of School Crime and Safety*, 2007, a report released in December 2006 by the U.S. Department of Education and the U.S. Department of Justice (see sidebar). Of the teachers surveyed, 3% reported being physically attacked in 2003-04. Teachers in central city schools were more likely to be threatened or physically attacked than teachers in urban fringe or rural schools.

Percent and Number of Teachers Who Faced Threats and Physical Attacks, 2003-04

	Teachers who reported they were threatened with injury		Teachers who reported they were physically attacked	
	Percent	Numbers	Percent	Numbers
All Teachers	6.8%	253,100	3.4%	127,100
City	10.0%	109,800	4.8%	52,800
Suburban	6.0%	78,100	3.2%	41,900
Town	5.4%	27,500	3.0%	15,500
Rural	4.7%	37,700	2.2%	17,700
Male	8.5%	78,500	2.6%	23,600
Female	6.3%	174,500	3.7%	104,000
Elementary	5.8%	113,700	4.5%	88,100
Secondary	8.0%	139,400	2.3%	39,500

Source: Indicators of School Crime and Safety, 2007, U.S. Department of Education, U.S. Department of Justice.

* * *

John Hammond, Middle School Teacher, New York

As a teenager, John Hammond coached his neighborhood little league team and worked as a day camp counselor. He knew he wanted to pursue a career that would allow him to work with kids and sports. When he attended high school in New York City in the early 1960s, he looked up to the physical education teacher, who drove to school in a black '61 Ford Falcon. He decided to become a physical education teacher. He wanted to make a difference in the lives of young people.

After graduation, he took a job in the mailroom of a financial corporation to pay for college, which he attended at night, majoring in physical education. He worked his way up to the credit and collections department at the company and was given his own accounts. Company executives wanted him to advance further, and they offered to send him to business school and pay for his education. But he wanted to be a teacher.

The teacher who supervised him during his student-teaching experience recommended him to a principal he knew at a junior high school in New York City. When he went to the school to interview for a position as a physical education teacher, the principal didn't ask any questions. He instantly offered Mr. Hammond the job and wanted him to start in February, the month after he was scheduled to graduate from college. Mr. Hammond was elated to have a job lined up immediately after graduation and considered himself lucky. "That feeling lasted about 10 minutes," he says.

Mr. Hammond was not aware at the time that the junior high school was new. When a new school opens in a district, the other schools typically send to the new school the students who are discipline problems and the students who have to repeat grade levels.

A student came to the school on one occasion with two steak knives and a snarling German shepherd. He was looking for the assistant principal who suspended him. The student went to the assistant principal's office, but he wasn't there. The office staff made an announcement over the public address system asking the assistant principal to come to his office. They also summoned another teacher, who was a former police officer, and two of the physical education teachers, including Mr. Hammond. When Mr. Hammond arrived, he was astonished at the scene. The teacher who used to be a police officer had the student pinned against the wall with the legs of a chair. The student jabbed at the air with the knives while the dog on the leash he held was growling viciously. Mr. Hammond turned to the other physical education teacher and said, "Does this happen often, because I didn't sign up for this. I didn't have a course for this in school."

Mr. Hammond's first class on Monday mornings was an eighth grade class that had between 40 and 60 boys in it. Some of them had been held back so many times they were 16 or 17 years old. The school had several vacant teaching positions so his assistant teacher was an individual with no physical education training. He was of no help to Mr. Hammond, a new teacher himself. Mr. Hammond was often confronted with brawls in the locker room and unruly behavior in the gym, and he struggled to manage the class. Every Sunday night he became physically ill as he anticipated the situation that awaited him first thing Monday morning.

After a couple of weeks, the boys' basketball coach had to take a leave of absence to undergo surgery. Previously, Mr. Hammond had spoken with the coach about his affinity for basketball, so the coach asked him to take over the team. That event turned out to be a turning point. Mr. Hammond strove to teach the players the game and to improve their teamwork and skills. After practice, he stayed and played a game of three-on-three with the kids. Because he respected the kids, treated them fairly, and impressed them with his own athletic abilities, he won their respect. The basketball players threatened the other students in the school to prevent them from giving him a hard time in physical education class. They warned the other students, "Don't mess with Mr. Hammond." After that, he was able to control the Monday morning class he previously dreaded, develop his skills as a teacher, and gain confidence in his ability to teach.

Mr. Hammond was tough but fair. He communicated his expectations to the students, but always with respect. If students were too loud and rowdy when lining up to go to the gymnasium, and they failed to heed his request for order and quiet, he didn't yell at them. He calmly and quietly asked the offending students to leave the line and go to his office, forcing them to miss their opportunity to have free play in the gym.

Soon he developed a camaraderie with about 10 other teachers who started around the same time as he did and had similar attitudes and approaches to teaching. After a while, he looked forward to going to school on Monday mornings. His ability to reach his students was rewarding. "You haven't taught until somebody learns something," he says.

Despite his rapport with most of the students, he continued to face disturbing incidents. One year, early in his career, he repeatedly admonished a student for disrupting his seventh grade health class. Finally, he gave the student an official notice to bring home. The student threatened Mr. Hammond, warning him that his cousin, a neighborhood gang leader, would be waiting to pummel him after school. Mr. Hammond reported the incident to the assistant principal, who reassured him that students frequently make idle threats but never follow through. Nevertheless, Mr. Hammond, who was still new to the school, spent the remainder of the day consumed by anxiety. Upon leaving the school building, he noticed a group of youths in the parking lot waiting for him. The leader approached him, eyed him with a glimmer of recognition, and uttered, "Mr. Hammond?" The boy had been one of Mr. Hammond's students the previous year and was a member of the school softball team Mr. Hammond coached. The gang leader turned to his cousin, the disruptive student in Mr. Hammond's health class, smacked him in the head, and firmly stated, "Don't you ever give this teacher any trouble again." Then he turned to Mr. Hammond and apologetically said, "I'm sorry, Mr. Hammond, it won't happen again."

Over the years, Mr. Hammond became more accustomed to the violence that surrounded his students and he became more comfortable handling precarious situations. When Mr. Hammond and a colleague, Robert Henderson, noticed an intruder had entered the school building, they began to approach him. The intruder exited the building and ran. Mr. Hammond and Mr. Henderson chased the intruder, who was several yards ahead. The intruder dropped something from his pocket and turned to retrieve it. When they noticed the object was a gun, they immediately turned around and continued running in the direction of the school building.

After Mr. Hammond became an assistant principal, he dealt with volatile situations within the school building more regularly. He often confiscated weapons from students. On one occasion, when a student was sent to his office because classmates had seen him with a razor blade, the student refused to admit that he had one. Mr. Hammond threatened to have the police come to the school and search the boy. The student finally revealed the razor blade, which was hidden in his mouth against his cheek. Mr. Hammond admitted he was surprised. Students often hid razor blades and knives in the linings of their jackets, but he had never seen a student conceal a razor blade in this manner before.

Mr. Hammond says students who got into trouble were usually the brightest—they were shrewd enough to get away with illicit acts and protect themselves from harm. Many students who engaged in behavior that violated not only school policy but also the law often had difficult backgrounds. However, a few of his students excelled academically despite their personal hardships. One of his students watched as her father, a drug dealer, was killed in a drive-by shooting while they were on their way to the grocery store. She later became valedictorian of her class. Another student lived with his grandmother because his father was killed and his mother was addicted to drugs. The student was accepted to a prestigious private high school and later an Ivy League university. Other students were not as fortunate.

One morning Mr. Hammond's colleague, Mr. Henderson, was watching the students file up the stairs near his office and noticed a red mark on the neck of one of the boys. He realized the student was bleeding from his neck; he had been sliced from ear to ear. Another teacher came over to help. "We sat holding the kid's neck together while I dialed 911," Mr. Henderson said. The student, an eighth grader, had been bullying a sixth grader, who produced a box cutter.

"He didn't even know he was cut," Mr. Henderson said. The incident "didn't stop him from being a bully," he said. The student was shot and killed a couple of years later. "He didn't learn," Mr. Henderson said. "The second time, he didn't make it."

* * *

Mary Williams, Elementary School Teacher, New York

Mary Williams taught at a private preschool after college for a year before taking a job teaching first grade at an elementary school in New York City. In her second year she had a boy in her class with severe behavior problems. On one occasion, after imploring him to stop coloring on the counter in the classroom and breaking crayons, Ms. Williams called the assistant principal's office for assistance. She was told she would receive a call back. When the phone rang, the student attempted to prevent Ms. Williams from answering it by shoving a chair against her legs and trapping her between the wall and the chair. She was able to pick up the phone just as she was being pinned against the wall.

The assistant principal's secretary relayed a message from the assistant principal to Ms. Williams: "She told me to deal with it," Ms. Williams says. After she moved the chair off of her, the student began to attack her—kicking and punching her. Then he began abusing the other students in the classroom. The school did not have a security guard, and Ms. Williams did not have a teaching assistant in her classroom. She ran into the hallway and began shouting for help. Another teacher heard her screams and came to her aid.

Ms. Williams had 29 students in her class, and much of her time was spent dealing with this particular student's disruptive and violent behavior. She contacted the student's mother, but she said the school should be doing more for her son. The administration expected Ms. Williams to deal with the student on her own.

Mid-way through the year, Ms. Williams decided not to return the following year. She said she had a similar situation with another student the previous year. She remained passionate about teaching, but she felt she couldn't handle the job anymore because it had become too dangerous.

But she returned to the school the next year because the position she was pursuing in another school district fell through. Her principal offered her a kindergarten ESL class instead of her first grade class and she accepted. "It was my only option if I wanted to continue teaching," she says. She was reluctant to return to preschool because she didn't want to take a large pay cut and relinquish her benefits and pension. But she was apprehensive. "The day before school I was hysterical," she says. She told herself that she would leave if she had another abusive student in her class. But her new position is working out. "I like my class. They are all pretty good kids," she says of the 27 students in her class.

"Looking back at last year, I don't know how I got through every day," she says, noting that her colleagues were all helpful and supportive. She says she took a personal day once in a while to recuperate from injuries she sustained from the student's abuse. "I will never do it again. I would have to quit," she says. "I would rather have no money and not eat than be abused again."

* * *

Jane Miller, Middle School Teacher, Florida

Jane Miller has been a middle school teacher for 11 years in Florida (see Chapter 3). She has experienced disruptive behavior that is violent or verbally offensive. One year she had an eighth grade boy in her class who entertained himself by imitating the wrestlers he frequently watched on television. He would turn classmates over and slam their heads into desks. Ms. Miller attempted to arrange conferences with the student's parents, but was unsuccessful. She reached out to the principal for help in dealing with the student, but he was unsupportive.

Ms. Miller had another student who was prone to violence in her sixth grade class. On the third day of school, she had to arrange a conference with the boy's parents because he was caught on a surveillance camera shoving another student into a wall. The student denied the image on the videotape was his. He had to be escorted to the restroom because he tended to push other students. His behavior continued throughout the year. Three weeks before the end of the year, he entered the classroom after visiting the bathroom and began pelting other students with balled-up paper towels. She asked the student to collect his books and leave the classroom. He responded by hurling his books across the room, knocking his desk over as he stood up, and knocking over three more desks and a trash can on his way out.

* * *

Michelle Anderson, Middle School Teacher, New York

Michelle Anderson has been teaching for six years in a New York suburb. In her sixth grade class, one student became hostile toward a classmate, slapping him on the back with a binder. Although the target walked away, the attacker's anger escalated and he began throwing things in the classroom. Concerned for the safety of her students, Ms. Anderson quickly got the students out of the classroom and called for the school psychologist and administrators. The student wrecked her classroom, throwing things off the desk and putting holes in the walls.

"I was very scared, but I held it together when the kids were with me. Once they left—luckily it was the last period of the day—I ended up crying in the bathroom," she says. "It really shook me up. It also made me realize how much the other kids were depending on me to protect them. It made me realize how dangerous teaching can be."

* * *

Deborah Clark, Elementary School Teacher, New York

Deborah Clark, a teacher in a New York suburb, was returning with her fourth grade class from a field trip. While boarding the bus, she reminded one of the boys of her rule that everyone must sit in the same seats that they occupied on the way to their destination. The boy brought his fist back and punched her in the stomach. When she called the boy's mother to inform her of the incident, she asked what Ms. Clark did to provoke her son. During a conference with the mother, Ms. Clark advised her she should make an effort to rein in her son's rebellious behavior before he gets himself into serious trouble. Years later, Ms. Clark read a news report that the boy, now 18, was arrested for drug possession and endangering the welfare of a minor because there were teenage girls in his car at the time.

* * *

Betty Robinson, Elementary School Teacher, New York

Betty Robinson taught special education in a private high school in New York City for nine years before teaching a self-contained special education class for fourth graders in another elementary school for one year. She had only 10 boys in her class, but seven were on medication for attention deficit hyperactivity disorder. They were a violent group and were constantly kicking and hitting her. She had to visit a hospital on one occasion because a student twisted her arm, causing a bad sprain. Another time she had to venture out onto a window ledge to retrieve a boy who climbed onto it.

At the end of the year, she found a job at a private school for special education students in a New York suburb, primarily because she wanted to work closer to where she and her husband had recently moved. In addition, she didn't like the atmosphere at the school in New York City. She says many of the veteran teachers were constantly yelling at the students, adding, "I didn't want to stay there because I didn't want to become them."

Chapter Six

The Truth About the 9-to-3 Job

"You're on from the time you walk into the building. You're on duty all the time. There's no free time. I wish I had a cubicle and I could switch to voice mail and get a breather."

Erin Baker, Middle School Teacher, Connecticut

The Workday

Denise Kramer, Elementary School Teacher, Colorado

Denise Kramer graduated from college with an undergraduate degree in elementary and special education. She enjoyed her student teaching experience, but she was turned off by some of the work associated with the job. All of the preparation that went into teaching elementary school, such as cutting, pasting and decorating bulletin boards, did not appeal to her. She decided she would be more interested in working for a non-profit group involved in advocacy work. After she graduated from college, she moved to Washington, D.C., to live with her sister. She decided to work part-time at a preschool "while I looked for a real job," she says.

"It was a wonderful choice that I didn't know I was making," she says. The school offered a cutting-edge early childhood education program, and the staff was professional and dedicated. "I fell in love with it again," she says of teaching.

The other teachers had extensive experience, and the atmosphere facilitated her professional growth. The staff was supportive, and they were receptive to her ideas about the program. When the school decided to launch a kindergarten program, they asked her to create the curriculum. "It was like a gift. Who gets to start a curriculum?" Because the school was privately funded, she had access to excellent resources and created an innovative reading program.

Ms. Kramer joined a local professional organization and met other teachers in D.C. She discovered that kindergarten teachers all over D.C. were struggling to teach reading because they lacked resources. She also found out that other programs contrasted with hers because they relied on insipid workbooks and worksheets. She started to feel as though she could make a positive contribution to the education field in the area of reading. She began volunteering as a tutor of bilingual reading and found the experience rewarding. She ultimately decided to return to school to become a certified reading specialist.

After spending two years at the private preschool/kindergarten and attaining her reading certification, Ms. Kramer and her boyfriend decided to move to Colorado. She is an outdoor enthusiast and yearned to live in a state where she could enjoy hiking and biking. But she found the market for teaching positions competitive. She applied for 80 jobs in Colorado and received only five responses. She was finally offered a position teaching reading at a middle school that had recently launched an ESL (English as a second language) program, which led to an influx of Hispanic students.

The overwhelming majority of Ms. Kramer's students are English-language learners. She has been at the school about two weeks and has already encountered a number of obstacles. She has about 70 students, and only seven parents attended back-to-school night. Based on the turnout, she anticipates a lack of parent involvement. She is considering home visits, but feels compelled to find a way to involve the parents in the school.

She's also aware of the attitude the other teachers harbor toward her. They have all worked at the school for many years, and they consider her to be naïve and idealistic, she says. "The teachers feel I'm green and I have no idea what it's really like."

The veteran teachers are not accustomed to teaching Hispanic students. Ms. Kramer has gotten the impression that they have low expectations for the students' academic achievement, an attitude she feels can be detrimental to the students' progress.

She is also concerned about the lack of interaction between students from different ethnic backgrounds. She thinks it would be beneficial for the different groups to socialize with one another. "They have an opportunity to learn from each other," she says. But she's not sure how to foster more interaction among the different groups. "I don't have any answers for how to get the kids to mix socially," she says. The school made a positive move by introducing an ESL program, "but they left out the social piece," she adds.

The attitude of the teachers toward her and her students, coupled with the student body's tendency toward self-segregation, creates an uncomfortable working environment for her. "The atmosphere doesn't feel so good to me, but it makes me want to stay," she says. She constantly ponders potential solutions for resolving the issues she faces. She thinks about how to encourage the parents of Hispanic students to become more involved in the school, how to facilitate more interaction among the students, and how to prompt the teachers to raise their expectations of the Hispanic students. She mulls it over while she's out running and while she's lying in bed at night. It's always on her mind.

She's eager to initiate positive changes at the school, but she's having a hard time formulating and implementing ideas because she's struggling to manage the day-to-day job. "In some ways I'm just trying to keep my head above water," she says.

She arrived in Colorado only a few days before school started, and entered her classroom for the first time two days before the first day of school. When she walked into her classroom, she saw there were no books. "I'm teaching reading with no books," she thought. "I had a minor heart attack."

She went to a used bookstore to stock up on books for her class. She also had to create a new reading curriculum because none existed before. She was hired to teach remedial reading, and only one of her reading classes was designated as an ESL class. But the large majority of her students are English-language learners, a situation she was not expecting. She also did not anticipate the volume of paperwork her job involves, such as completing student evaluations, filling out forms, organizing a filing system and ordering supplies.

She arrives at school at 6:45 a.m., nearly two hours before the students, and she leaves at 6 p.m. School ends at 3:30 p.m., but some of her students stay until 4 p.m. so that she can verify that they did their reading assignments in lieu of a parent's signature.

Ms. Kramer had hoped to avoid taking work home so she could have time in the evenings to decompress. But she has been forced to work at home in the evenings because of all of the preparation involved with launching a new program. She also has to read the books her students are reading. The level of work she takes home will have to taper off at some point, she says, "or I'll start to go crazy." She has been at the school for only two weeks and she's already exhausted, she says.

* * *

Nearly 50% of new teachers leave the profession within the first five years, according to the National Education Association (NEA). Teachers who do not plan to remain in the profession until retirement cite unsatisfactory working conditions and low pay as the primary reasons, the NEA says. Resignations among certified teachers in New York City (for reasons other than retirement or problems with licensure) reached a record high of 4,303 in 2006, up 69% since 2001, the United Federation of Teachers (UFT) announced in November 2007. Nearly 14% of new teachers hired in the 2006-07 school year have already resigned, the UFT reported.

Working conditions, rather than salaries, are to blame for the exodus of New York City's teachers. Teacher salaries in New York City have increased 43% in the past five years, helping to attract and retain better-educated and more qualified teachers. "But now we must do more to keep good teachers," said Randi Weingarten, president of the UFT, in a press release dated November 19, 2007. Weingarten noted that the system is losing more than one-third of new teachers within their first three years and nearly half within six years. These statistics haven't changed since 2000, but now the city is losing more veteran teachers as well. According to a UFT study in 2006, new teachers said they would be more likely to stay if they had better working conditions, such as smaller class sizes, more collaboration with and support from school administrators, and greater availability of equipment and supplies. They also said they would be encouraged to stay if they were given more latitude to teach what they felt their students needed to learn rather than preparing them for standardized tests.

The NEA says it is a myth that teachers work six-hour days and enjoy summers off. Teachers work an average of nine to 10 hours a day during the school year, when grading papers, lesson preparation, and advising extracurricular clubs are factored in, the NEA says. Furthermore, teachers spend summers working second jobs, teaching summer school, and taking classes to fulfill certification renewal requirements and to advance their careers. Teachers return to the classroom in late August or early September to begin setting up their classrooms.

* * *

Andrea Turner, Elementary School Teacher, Florida

Andrea Turner has been a teacher for 30 years. She began teaching the day after she graduated from college at the school where she student taught in New York City. She taught pre-K for six months before moving to New Jersey to take a position teaching first grade. She worked at the school in New Jersey for six years, then she took nine years off to raise her children. When her sons were older, she moved to Texas and taught kindergarten through third grade for 12 years. She finally settled in Florida after her sons went off to college and she got divorced. She has been teaching kindergarten through second grade in Florida for 12 years.

"I've forever been in love with my profession," she says about teaching. She was surprised by her passion for teaching because she did not intend to become an educator. She majored in foreign language in college and planned to pursue a career in the diplomatic field. She took education courses to satisfy her father, who wanted her to become a teacher. It was during her stint as a student-teacher that she "fell in love with it," she says.

She currently teaches kindergarten in a lower-income community in Florida. "It is so all-consuming," she says of her job. "I feel an enormous responsibility, being responsible for so many little lives."

She begins preparing for the upcoming school year in July by going to the copy store and duplicating handouts. She knows she will not have time to accomplish this task in August because she will have to unpack, set up her room and attend meetings before school begins. She calls her home "school central" in the weeks leading up to the first day of school because she is busy organizing school supplies and preparing for the year ahead. At the end of each school year, she has to pack up her entire room into boxes and stack the boxes so the floors can be waxed.

To handle her workload during the school year, she takes work home at night and spends time during the weekends on long-term planning and lesson planning. She teaches 20 to 25 students each year without support from a teaching assistant or aide. She spends about $1,000 on her classroom each year for snacks and materials. She's not allowed to ask the parents to contribute funds for classroom supplies.

Kindergarten today is akin to first grade in prior years, she says. The kindergarten day used to consist primarily of playtime, but today teachers are expected to incorporate literacy—reading and writing—into most activities. (See "A Day in the Life" later in this chapter for a breakdown of Ms. Turner's typical day.)

In addition to managing a heavy workload, she often deals with behavior issues. One year she had a boy in her class who would pick things up and hurl them across the room when he became upset. She knew the child probably required special services because of his severe behavior problems, but the process was slow. Streams of experts visited her classroom to observe the child during the year because documentation was required to support a request for special education services. The boy was not placed in a class for students with severe behavior issues until the following year.

While teaching in New Jersey, a boy in her first grade class would threaten the other children with violence. He would take a pair of scissors and tell the other kids he was going to stab them.

The behavior issues, the heavy workload, and the long hours don't bother Ms. Turner as much as the lack of compensation she receives. She says it took her 30 years as a teacher to reach the same salary level at which her son started when he graduated from law school. She has seen teachers become disgruntled because their salaries are not commensurate with their workloads and dedication. "If we all had an aide and good salary, it would be paradise," she says.

Although her job is demanding, Ms. Turner enjoys it because of the children. "They're just fabulous and wonderful. They energize me," she says. The kindergarten environment also appeals to her. "It's a microcosm of the world," she says, because children from different backgrounds "gel into a community." The amusing things her young students say and do keep her spirits elevated. "It's hysterical in there," she says of her classroom.

But her impact on future generations is perhaps the job's greatest reward, she says. "Someday I'll look back on life and say, 'I made a difference.'"

* * *

Valerie Edwards, Middle School Teacher, Georgia

Unlike some of her colleagues, Valerie Edwards did not aspire to be a teacher when she was attending college. "I wasn't one of those people who knew from when they were younger that they wanted to be a teacher. I sort of just fell into it," she says. The subject she gravitated toward was Spanish. She enjoyed her Spanish courses and achieved strong grades. She decided to immerse herself in the language and culture of Spain by studying there for a semester during her junior year. "It was probably the most incredible five months of my life, and I can't say enough good things about it," she says.

When she returned to college for the second semester of her junior year, she felt pressure to select a major, but she was still ambivalent about a career path. "But I knew I loved Spanish, and after my trip, I also loved the culture." She met with her guidance counselor, who reviewed her transcript and determined she needed only six more credits to complete a Spanish major, primarily due to the credits that transferred from her semester in Spain. After she decided to major in Spanish, she began to consider how she could use her degree to land a job after graduation. She figured she had two options—business and teaching.

"So I registered for a couple of introductory education courses. Before I knew it, I was signing up for student-teaching and on my way to being a teacher," she says. "It was pretty scary, actually, because I remember it all happening so fast, and at one point I just stopped and thought, 'Wait a minute, am I actually doing this? Am I really going to be a Spanish teacher?'"

She did her student-teaching in an urban district in Maryland, spending half a semester at a middle school and half at a high school. "It was pretty rough there," she says. "But when it was over, I felt so proud, and I knew that after teaching [there] I could teach anywhere."

After she graduated from college, she accepted a position teaching Spanish at a middle school in a wealthy New York suburb, a sharp contrast to the urban setting she experienced previously. She spent three years at the school, teaching primarily sixth and seventh grade (her first year she taught one high school class).

The pressure on the teachers to be "not just good, but great" was enormous at the school, she says. The expectations were high because the school had an excellent reputation, and she felt she had to perform as well as the veteran teachers in the foreign language department. The department had a solid reputation, and she strove to live up to the standards that had been set by her colleagues. She also felt pressure to thoroughly prepare her students for the New York State Spanish exam that is administered to eighth graders. The district would be expecting the students to achieve high scores on the exam.

Dealing with parents caused her the most anxiety. "It felt as if the parents ran the school," she says. "I always felt like I was walking on egg shells when it came to calling a parent or having a conference because I knew being on the parent's good side meant a good chance of keeping your job." She felt she needed the parents' support to receive tenure. "I couldn't believe how intense they were though," she says. Parents often called her to question why their children received an A and not an A+. "It was crazy," she says.

Despite the pressure, Ms. Edwards loved her job in New York. But after three years, she moved to Georgia to be with her fiancé, who was stationed at a U.S. military base there. Georgia represented a completely different experience, once again. "It's like a whole different world down here," she says. She's been in Georgia for about three months teaching sixth, seventh and eighth grade Spanish. Spanish is considered a "connections" course at her new school. It is not considered a core subject, but an elective such as chorus, band, home economics and careers.

The most stressful aspect of her job in Georgia has been adjusting to new routines and learning new policies and procedures. "It's also just stressful in general to be a new teacher," she says. "I felt like for the entire first month—and sometimes this still happens—I'd learn something new every day, but I'd learn it the hard way." For example, she sent a student to the nurse without first filling out an official form that had to be printed from the shared computer network.

Ms. Edwards doesn't have her own classroom. All of her materials sit on a large cart on wheels that she has to push to three different classrooms during the day. She teaches two classes in each room, for a total of six. "It's pretty annoying, especially trying to get though the crowded hallways in between classes, but I guess I'm getting used to it, and it keeps me organized," she says.

The cart has a compact disc player so that she can sing songs to her class. "I'm praying the other teachers don't stay in their rooms while I'm teaching because I'll be so embarrassed singing those songs in front of them," she says.

She is a big proponent of "do now" activities, and not having her own classroom makes administering these assignments challenging. [A "do now" activity is a daily review activity that is already up on the board when the students enter the room. As soon as they enter, they sit down and immediately start on the activity. It typically takes about five minutes. The "do now" activity helps the students adhere to a routine and encourages them to focus on something immediately. It also affords her time to pass papers back or handle issues that arise at the beginning of class, such as students who approach her because they don't have a pencil, lost their homework, or were absent the previous day and want to know what they missed.] Since she doesn't have her own classroom and can't put the "do now" activity on the board, she had to conceive of a new system. Her fiancé suggested she put the activity on a small, portable white board. She purchased one at an office supply store. "It's not quite the same because I have to fit the activity on such a small space, but it gets the job done," she says.

Her schedule requires her to teach for three hours straight in the morning. After a break, she teaches for another hour and a half in the afternoon. She has to trek across the entire school with her cart to get to her sixth grade class from her eighth grade class. During her break, she is occasionally required to sell ice cream in the cafeteria.

The faculty does not have a lunchroom, and they are expected to eat in the student cafeteria. Feeling uncomfortable with this set up and desiring a quiet break from students, she asked a colleague if she could eat lunch in her office. She got the impression from her coworker's reaction that eating lunch in her office would be unacceptable. "She kind of made a face like she had to think about it, but she seemed weird about it." She asked her colleague where she should eat. "She said the cafeteria, so I went there and it was complete chaos."

All of the teachers are required to walk their classes to the cafeteria and eat there at a separate table. She sat and ate with a few of them. Then she discussed the situation with another connections teacher. She and the other connections teachers decided that if they bring lunch they will eat in the home economics teacher's room. But if they buy lunch in the cafeteria, they will stay there.

Ms. Edwards has also learned that taking a sick day or a personal day does not involve a simple phone call to the office. She is responsible for finding a substitute teacher to take over her classes. She has to log onto a website that lists phone numbers for people who have agreed to serve as substitute teachers in her county. Then she has to call the people on the list until she finds someone to take the job. She must fill out a form online and contact the main office to inform them a substitute will be taking her place that day.

The school has a unified grading system that teachers must adhere to. She's not permitted to grade homework, a policy she finds unusual.

She is also trying to adjust to the "parent portal." Parents who sign up for the parent portal can view their child's grades online. "It's stressful for teachers because one, we have to make sure we're constantly updating our grades on the computer, and two, it gives parents more reasons to call and ask questions," she says. "I get e-mails and phone calls like 'Why does it say my son has a zero on the numbers activity?' and I have to explain that it's because he didn't do it." The benefit of the portal is that parents are informed if their children aren't completing their assignments. But it is time-consuming for teachers.

The athletic director, who is also Ms. Edwards' mentor, asked her to coach the cheerleading squad. Soon after accepting the role, she began to regret it. "The whole reason I came to Georgia was to spend more time with my fiancé, especially before he deploys to Iraq in a few months, but coaching takes up so much time," she says. She also feels bad that her new puppy is stuck in a crate until at least 5 p.m. every day.

She accepted the coaching position because she felt pressured. When the word spread that she was considering coaching the cheerleading squad, colleagues started to approach her to tell her how excited they were. "As a new teacher, I wanted to make a good impression and felt like I'd be letting a lot of people down if I didn't." She knew she would be working closely with the athletic director and didn't want to disappoint her.

She said the compensation she was offered for the coaching job did not impact her decision to accept it. "The money is unbelievably awful," she says.

Aside from the hours, the job itself isn't bad, she says. "The girls on the squad are sweet for the most part, and they're really talented." When she accepted the job, the athletic director allowed her to shorten the practice time to 45 minutes, three days a week. But once a week there is a game at 5 p.m. If it's an away game, she has to travel at least an hour and a half. Most game days she doesn't get home until at least 8 p.m. She hired a dog walker.

"Overall it's just exhausting," she says. "Between teaching six classes a day, coaching until 4:30 p.m. and coming home to a puppy, I feel like it's never-ending chaos. I have no idea how people are teachers plus coaches while also raising children."

* * *

Elizabeth Walker, Elementary School Teacher, Missouri

Elizabeth Walker has been teaching for about 10 years in Missouri. She started teaching after graduating from college. She became a teacher because "I loved school," she says. "I loved the idea of being able to continually be challenged with new students and new ideas. I also loved that the education system values educating their teachers as well. I wanted to work with children, and I enjoyed the positive attitude that the job brought."

Ms. Walker, who teaches second grade, receives calls from parents every day. Calls come in as early as 7 a.m. and as late as 7 p.m. They contact her at home after hours. To reduce the number of calls she receives at home, she has stopped giving out her home phone number. Some parents call her on a regular basis to check up on their child or to inform her of every minor detail. Divorced parents request separate parent-teacher conferences. In one child's case, both parents (who were divorced) called her every day to find out how their child was doing.

"There is less trust in the classroom teacher than there used to be," she says. Yet some parents expect her to deal with their child's social and emotional issues, not just their academic needs. If a child goes home and complains that a classmate doesn't like him or her, the parents will call her and ask her to handle it instead of advising their child on how to deal with the situation.

Parents expect their children to assume less responsibility than in the past, she says. They call her to find out when a test is scheduled or if a study guide is available.

On the other end of the spectrum, there are children who require parental intervention, but don't receive it. She had a student who informed others he planned to kill himself, but his parents never called.

While some of the parents she deals with are demanding, others go out of their way to help, she notes.

Ms. Walker must purchase her own supplies because she is not provided with the teaching materials she needs. She purchased leveled readers for reading instruction and silent reading. She is not provided with science textbooks or math textbooks to guide her lessons. She is expected to assemble the resources she will use for her lessons in those subject areas, and purchase them with her own money. When parents come into the classroom for parties or other events, they often casually remove supplies that she purchased from her desk, such as pencils, pens and scissors. As she watches supplies leave her desk, she grows concerned that parents will inadvertently take or misplace them.

Teachers at her school are expected to handle students with a variety of academic, behavioral and mental health issues, she says. Her students' skill levels are diverse—she has students who are barely reading and others who are reading well above their grade level. Out of the 26 students in her class this year, 10 have some type of special need, even though she teaches a regular education class. She had a student in her class one year who was suffering from bipolar disorder. She does not receive support from a special education teacher or a teaching assistant, and she does not have a degree in special education. If a student with a severe special need, such as mental retardation or autism, is placed in a regular education class, a teaching assistant will be assigned to the class on some days. The teaching assistants float among classes where they are needed, so they are available to each class only on certain days.

Teachers have multiple responsibilities, from supervising extracurricular activities, to taking staff development classes, to serving on committees. Ms. Walker serves on five committees, such as the Positive Behavior Support Committee and the Abilities Awareness Committee.

Most people assume teachers work about six hours a day because that is the length of the school day, she says. But teachers typically arrive two hours early to check voice mail and e-mail and prepare lessons. They grade papers and prepare lessons when they go home at the end of the day.

"It's not a job, it's a lifestyle," she says.

She tries to multitask and work as efficiently as possible. She copes with the stress by sharing her experiences with others, leaving as much work as possible at school, and staying physically fit through exercise. "It certainly helps to have a supportive team here at work and an understanding husband who allows me to gripe," she says. Despite the pressures, she loves her job "when I actually get to teach."

Although she enjoys teaching, she plans to resign at the end of the school year. She is pregnant with her second child. "I know that with the additional pressure and the ever-increasing demands put on me here at school that I am not a nice person by the time I get home," she says. "If I would be able to simply continue to come to work on time, do my actual job, and then go home, I would love to be able to keep working. But, unfortunately, I know that that is not what will happen now or in the future."

* * *

Heather Dalton, New York, South Carolina and California

Heather Dalton became a teacher because she has always enjoyed working with children. She worked as a camp counselor growing up and during college. After graduating from college, she started teaching at a New York City elementary school. She taught kindergarten for two years and first grade for two years.

The administration expected the teaching staff to arrive at least a half an hour early and stay well after dismissal to plan lessons and set up for the next day. She often stayed until 9 p.m. and ordered in dinner with her colleagues. The principal and assistant principal also stayed. "It was expected," she says.

She was able to handle the long hours at the time because she was young and didn't have a family. "Now there is no way I'd be able to do it," she says. Most of the teachers were just starting out like her, but some had families and found the hours burdensome.

Before she started working, she had an idealistic view of the teaching profession. She expected the teachers and administrators to work together as partners. She thought she would have an amiable, collaborative relationship with the principal. But she soon discovered the principal was clearly in charge. "The principal is not your ally," she says. "The principal is your boss."

She was also surprised by her interactions with the parents of the students in her class. Many of the parents were her age (22 years old) or younger, and they frequently asked her for parenting advice. She wasn't a parent at the time, but she did her best to respond to their questions. She suggested they establish rules and strive for consistency. They asked her how to discipline their kids at home.

After four years in New York City, Ms. Dalton moved to South Carolina and taught first grade for four years in a low-income, rural district. Her job in South Carolina brought more surprises. She was astonished by the prejudice that still existed in the south, even in children as young as six. "They would bring it into the classroom," she says. For instance, a child might say he or she couldn't play with or sit with another child because the other child belonged to a different race. But most of the children were taught to respect her and listen to her because she was their teacher.

She was also shocked by the school's use of corporal punishment. The assistant principal, who was responsible for administering the punishment, would strike children on the bottom with a paddle. The assistant principal once asked Ms. Dalton to come into her office because she needed a witness. Ms. Dalton refused. She never sent a student to the assistant principal's office for discipline. She was thankful that the next school in South Carolina where she worked did not administer corporal punishment because the principal was opposed to it.

She moved to California and taught a fourth and fifth grade combination class for one year before becoming a stay-at-home mother to her son for five years. Last year she returned to work as a part-time reading specialist for kindergarten through fifth grade. She works two days a week. Attempting to obtain a teaching license in California has been a frustrating experience. Although she has a master's degree and a teaching license in New York and South Carolina, she has had to enroll in classes and take tests to receive certification in California. She is displeased that the classes and the exams are stealing her time from her family.

* * *

Erin Baker, Middle School Teacher, Connecticut

Erin Baker has been teaching middle school English in Connecticut for 12 years. She decided to reduce her hours and work part-time this year because she has an 18-month-old child and "teaching is exhausting." She felt she didn't have enough energy to devote to both her job and her child.

"You're a nurse, psychologist, mom, dad, everything," she says. "It's very draining dealing with the needs of children."

It is a widespread misconception that teaching is well-suited for mothers, she says. While this notion might apply to mothers of school-age children because they share the same hours, mothers of babies and preschoolers face enormous difficulties juggling their families and work lives.

Her biggest challenge as a teacher is the lack of down time. "You're on from the time you walk into the building," she says. "You're on duty all the time. There's no free time. I wish I had a cubicle and I could switch to voice mail and get a breather."

Because she is an English teacher, grading is time-consuming. She has 100 students, and therefore 100 essays to grade at a time. She has had to pay a babysitter so she could devote time to grading papers. "I began to say, I'm killing myself. I'm working so hard and I'm not earning the big bucks."

Ms. Baker started her own business because it will afford her more flexible hours. She's hoping it will develop into a full-time job eventually, allowing her to leave the teaching profession entirely. But until her business takes off, she's keeping her part-time teaching position because her family needs the income.

Parents in the affluent community where she works have high expectations for their children. She says having a conversation with the parent of an average student is difficult. When her eighth graders are informed in April whether or not they were placed in advanced high school English, she has to have uncomfortable talks with the parents of the students who were rejected. She also finds it difficult to tell parents that their B student will probably never be an A student. She chooses her words carefully when speaking with parents. But she feels that becoming a parent herself will further improve her ability to communicate with parents about sensitive issues.

Ms. Baker interacts with parents constantly because of e-mail and voice mail. She receives messages from parents every day. The constant demands for time and attention from parents, on top of all of the other stresses, "can put a teacher over the top," she says.

Despite the pressures of her job, she remains enthusiastic about it because she enjoys working with children. She enjoys discussing literature with her students and listening to them share their writing. When teachers treat students with respect, rather than condescension, they respond better, she says. Former students keep in touch with her and come back to visit. She also appreciates the support the school receives from the parents, who volunteer their time to benefit the students and staff.

She remains positive about her job by associating with teachers who share her attitude. Not all of them do, she says. She advises new teachers not to eat in the faculty room to avoid being influenced by the negativity exuded there. "There are teachers who make obnoxious comments" about students and parents, she notes. She never eats in the faculty room herself. She usually works during lunch and prep periods to limit the work she takes home as much as possible.

* * *

Alice Daniels, Elementary School Teacher, New York

Alice Daniels always knew she wanted to be a teacher. At the age of 73, she remains committed to the profession. "I knew it was a low-prestige career and it was a low-paying career. I was fortunate that I didn't have to worry about that," she says. When she was in school, she used to accompany her mother to her teaching job when she had a day off and her mother did not. She got to watch the class sometimes if her mother had to step out of the room. She embarked on her own teaching career after she graduated from college in the 1950s and continues to teach today.

Ms. Daniels spent much of her career teaching fifth and sixth grade in a socio-economically diverse school district in New York State. After 17 years at the school, she accepted a position running the gifted program in an affluent school district in New York. She left after three years because "the principal and I didn't see eye to eye," she says. "He felt I was giving the gifted kids too much work, and they shouldn't have to do work; it should be fun."

After attaining her doctorate in education, she began teaching education courses at different colleges. She always knew that she would not teach young children full-time for her entire career. "Teaching, if you're doing it right, is exhausting," she says. She raised four children while teaching. "My kids complained that I used up all of my energy and patience on my kids in school," she says.

The most tiring aspect of the job is that "you're always on," she says. "It's like being on stage for the full performance," she says. "You can't be in a bad mood or the kids will pick up on it." The job didn't end for her at dismissal time. She brought work home, such as planning lessons and grading papers.

This year she plans to volunteer, part-time, at a school in New York City. She doesn't know exactly what she'll be doing yet, but she's willing to take on whatever task the principal assigns her. "I do everything," she says.

Looking back on her long career, Ms. Daniels says she doesn't remember it being all that difficult, although discipline was always a problem for her. "I was never a good disciplinarian," she says. "When I tried to be, they didn't believe me."

The worst experience she had was when one of the boys in her class attempted to attack another boy. She grabbed the boy, who was about 200 pounds, and wound up flipping over his shoulder and landing on the floor. "He was a scary kid," she says. But it was more difficult to deal with the student's mother. When the student forced a classmate to steal $50 from Ms. Daniels' wallet, the student's mother refused to believe it.

Although she experienced a few distressing incidents involving parents, she didn't face anything she couldn't handle. "A parent bad-mouthed me to other parents, but it wears off and it's not such a big deal," she says.

Ms. Daniels didn't face many difficulties with parents over the years because she made an effort to work with them and listen to their input, even in her early years as a teacher. "That's something I've always believed in," she says.

A few of her college students told her that many of their classmates were pursuing lucrative careers. Their classmates questioned why they were becoming teachers when they could make more money doing something else. "But we're the ones who are so excited about working because we love what we do," they told her.

"They're just making money."

* * *

A Day in the Life

Kindergarten Teacher Andrea Turner's Typical Day

- ◆ Wakes at 5 a.m. to exercise before leaving for work.

- ◆ Arrives at work at 7 a.m.

- ◆ Begins each morning with the children engaging in independent activities at the tables while she handles administrative matters, such as attendance, filing, checking homework books, grading and assessments.

- ◆ Holds the "morning meeting" which includes the calendar and calendar math, modeled writing and shared "big book" reading.

- ◆ Escorts the children to their special, such as art and music. While the children are at their special for 30 minutes, she scrambles to complete a series of tasks, including checking e-mail, voice mail and her mailbox in the office.

- ◆ Provides a snack for the children because they have a late lunch. Usually she has a jar of animal crackers in the classroom. She doesn't ask the children to bring in their own snacks to make sure snack time is quick and fair. Some parents have offered to supply snacks for the class this year. To avoid wasting time, during snack she uses an overhead projector to practice high-frequency words and sight words.

- ◆ Sends the children to the classroom literacy centers, where they rotate among three activities, each one involving different literacy-based activities, such as reading, writing words and illustrating personal dictionaries.

- Conducts 30 minutes of physical education, which she says she's required to do. She incorporates learning into the activity (e.g., alphabet jumping jacks—a is for apple, b is for boy, etc.).

- Escorts the children to the cafeteria for their 30-minute lunch period. "I run back to my room and gobble down my lunch. Hopefully I have time to go to the bathroom that day," she says.

- Picks the children up at lunch, takes them outside, and supervises their recess period.

- Spends 10 minutes helping the children empty sand from their shoes and tie their shoelaces.

- Lines the children up in the hall for drinks.

- Begins the afternoon with five minutes of quiet time, during which she plays soft music and she lets them wipe their hands with baby wipes (she calls them kid wipes) because there is no time to have them all line up at the sink to wash their hands.

- Presents a math lesson using the "big book." The children complete worksheets that match the "big book." She says she would prefer to use manipulatives for math but there's no time.

- Reads a story to close the day.

- Passes out the homework books.

- Escorts the children outside to meet the buses.

- Escorts the 15 car riders to their cars.

- Waits for the buses to leave. The dismissal process takes about 20 to 25 minutes.

- Returns to her classroom to prepare for the next day and attend to administrative matters, such as grading papers, placing them in the children's mailboxes, preparing and printing worksheets for the next day, responding to e-mail, responding to voice mail and returning phone calls from parents.

- Holds parent-teacher conferences and attends meetings.
- Finishes work at about 5 p.m.
- Sets aside two days during the month of October for evening conferences from 8 p.m. and 9 p.m. to accommodate working parents.

* * *

Sixth Grade Teacher Sarah Brown's Typical Day
(Ms. Brown recorded the following events as they occurred on one particular day.)

- **7:15 a.m.:** Arrives at school and sets up the classroom for a lesson involving individual manipulatives for each student.
- **7:50–8:34 a.m.: First Period/Math Class.** Presents the algebra lesson. The students find it difficult to refrain from touching the manipulatives while she is demonstrating. They constantly stack, drop and play with the pieces.
- **8:37–9:17 a.m.: Second Period/Preparation Time.** Responds to two parent e-mails and grades tests from the previous day.
- **9:20–10:00 a.m.: Third Period/Math Class.** Presents the algebra lesson.
- **10:03–10:43 a.m.: Fourth Period/Math Class.** Presents the algebra lesson.
- **10:46–11:26 a.m.: Fifth Period/Lunch.** She rarely eats lunch with her colleagues because during her lunch period she has to give students extra help, re-teach a lesson to students who were absent, or give retests. Today 13 students come in to take a retest. The students ask numerous questions during the test, which is typical. Other students who have lunch during fifth period enter the classroom to ask her questions and distract the test takers. She attempts

to continue grading tests from the day before as she fields questions.

◆ **11:29 a.m.–12:09 p.m.: Sixth Period/Preparation Time.** Visits the main office to submit the paperwork for a teacher conference. A parent of one of her students happens to be in the office and corners her. After about 15 minutes of paperwork and talking to the parent, she returns to her classroom. She has 20 minutes to use the bathroom, heat up her lunch and eat it. She manages to eat half of her lunch while grading the retests.

◆ **12:12–12:52 p.m.: Seventh Period/Math Class.** Presents the algebra lesson.

◆ **12:55–1:35 p.m.: Eighth Period/Preparation Time.** Calls a parent. During fourth period, a student handed her a note in which his father requested Ms. Brown call him. He says he believes his son answered a question correctly on a test, but she took two points off. She explains to the father why she had to give his son partial credit and deduct the two points. After the conversation, she responds to an e-mail from another parent. She finishes her lunch and begins preparing for the following day.

◆ **1:38–2:18 p.m.: Ninth period/Math Strategies Class.** Presents a lesson on solving word problems and explaining solutions in writing. Students have the misconception that math doesn't involve writing, and she has to stress that showing their work is important.

◆ **2:18 p.m.: After school.** Finishes preparing for the following day and grades homework and "do nows" for about 80 students. To keep the material fresh in the minds of her students, she has a three-minute "do now" assignment every class that consists of two computation questions covering past material. She grades them that day and returns them the following day. For the students who made mistakes, she provides the correct solution and an explanation of how to arrive at the solution. She requires the students to redo the problem if they made mistakes, to explain their mistakes in words, and to show their work to arrive at the correct answer. If they complete these tasks, they receive half-credit for the assignment. Ms. Brown typically grades tests and quizzes after school as well. She also plans lessons, and designs tests and quizzes. She enters all of the grades into her grade book.

- ♦ **4:15 p.m.: Leaves school.** She brings home the rest of the retests to grade.

- ♦ **That evening: Checks e-mail.** Ms. Brown receives e-mails from three parents and responds to them. Ms. Brown responds to parent e-mails in the evening to avoid spending her preparation periods addressing e-mails.

* * *

The Compensation

Teachers draw an average salary of between $49,000 and $51,000 annually, according to figures from the U.S. Department of Labor, Bureau of Labor Statistics. Teachers make less than computer programmers, nurses, insurance agents and a number of other professionals (see sidebar).

The average increase in teacher salaries trailed behind the rate of inflation in the 2005-06 school year, according to a study by the NEA. The NEA reported that public school teacher salaries increased an average of 2.9%, compared to a 3.9% increase in the rate of inflation. Over the past 10 years, the average salary for public school teachers increased only 1.3% after adjusting for inflation, according to the NEA. Public school teachers were paid $49,026 on average in the

2005-06 school year.

The American Federation of Teachers (AFT) reported a similar trend. An AFT study determined that in 2004-05 teachers earned an average salary of $47,602, a 2.2% increase from 2003-04. The increase was not enough to keep pace with inflation or the earnings of other workers in the private or public sectors, according to the AFT. The starting salary for teachers averaged $31,753 in 2004-05.

The research on teacher compensation indicates new teachers are often unable to repay their student loans or afford houses in the communities where they teach. According to the NEA, hundreds of thousands of college students go into debt to become teachers.

"They can't afford to repay their student loans on a teacher's salary," said Anthony Daniels, chairperson of the NEA Student Program, at a conference. Daniels' remarks were quoted in an NEA press release. "Studies show the main reason cited by those who quit teaching is the difficulty in making ends meet. We are losing too many good teachers, and it's costing our children," Daniels said.

Average Annual Salary, 15 Occupations

Occupation	Mean Annual Wage Estimate
Computer Programmers	$69,500
Occupational Therapists	$62,510
Accountants and Auditors	$60,670
Landscape Architects	$60,480
Registered Nurses	$59,730
Insurance Sales Agents	$58,450
Flight Attendants	$56,150
Advertising Sales Agents	$51,370
Secondary School Teachers**	**$51,150**
Middle School Teachers**	**$49,470**
Elementary School Teachers*	**$48,700**
Interior Designers	$48,000
Electricians	$46,620
Paralegals and Legal Assistants	$45,460
Child, Family, School Social Workers	$40,640

*Excludes special education; ** Excludes special education and vocational education. Source: May 2006 National Occupational Employment and Wage Estimates, U.S. Dept. of Labor, Bureau of Labor Statistics.

* * *

Kathy Moore, Elementary School Teacher, California

Kathy Moore has always wanted to be a teacher. "It is my calling," she says. "The reason I decided to become a teacher is because it is who I am. I know that sounds contrived, but it is true." She smiles when her young daughters tell people they want to become teachers too.

Ms. Moore graduated from college with a liberal studies degree with an emphasis on elementary education. She has a master's degree in curriculum and instruction. She has taught sixth grade in the same California school district for 10 years.

She teaches in the community where she grew up. She is devoted to her students and enjoys the rich rewards of her profession. She has been nominated for Teacher of the Year in her school district. When asked by the nominating committee what she brings to her job, her answer was she gives her time. She is always working—she thinks about her next lesson in her car, does research at home on the Internet, prepares and plans for class on the weekends. "It's constantly on my mind," she says.

She created a garden on the school grounds, not only to beautify the property, but also to foster relationships between the community and the school. Residents and businesses have donated time and money to the garden. Her efforts have facilitated interaction between local business and government leaders and students, offering students a glimpse of the real world and potential role models.

Ms. Moore yearns to be a part of the community where she teaches—where she grew up—but she and her husband, who is also a teacher, are struggling to find a way to afford a home there. They have two daughters and currently live in a 700-square-foot apartment about 22 miles from where she works.

It has been years since she received a cost-of-living raise. The teachers' union is fighting for a cost of living increase but has reached an impasse with the school district, and she and the other teachers are working without a contract. The teachers have the option of striking, but refuse because a strike would adversely affect their students.

"I'm so heartbroken that I can't buy a home at an affordable price in my own hometown," she says.

* * *

Joan Phillips, Elementary School Teacher, Florida

Joan Phillips has worked in the education field for 12 years, three as a teacher (see Chapter 3). Prior to attaining her teaching position at an elementary school in Florida, she was an aide and a teacher's assistant. She's 37 years old, and she's not sure if she will be able to do her job for another 30 years because of the energy and time commitment required. She is more concerned about supporting herself on her teacher's salary.

Teachers in her district have a 10-month contract, which means she doesn't have an income during the summer. She needs to obtain a summer job to pay her bills during that time. Every year, she begins searching for summer employment in January, which is a stressful process. Most private sector employers are reluctant to hire an applicant just for the summer. This year, she was lucky to find a job teaching summer school for four weeks.

Ms. Phillips calls all of the companies to which she owes money to ask if she can defer payment until the fall, or if they can offer her a discounted rate. She worked out an arrangement that cut her monthly car payments in half, but extended the life of the loan.

She lives with her mother and supports her. Her mother collects Social Security. "We just make it," she says.

She doesn't expect her financial situation to improve because pay increases are not readily awarded in her district. "Every year we have to fight for our raise," she says. "It's sad because it's not a lot of money. It shouldn't have to be this way."

Despite her financial insecurity, she plans to stay with the job. "I don't know what I would do if I left. I don't have any other interests."

* * *

Certification Requirements

Aspiring teachers must go through a rigorous and expensive

process to become certified to teach. To maintain their certification, teachers typically have to enroll in continuing education courses or attend staff development programs. According to the AFT, prospective teachers are required to obtain at least a bachelor's degree, usually in a field related to the subject they plan to teach, and most states also require some type of advanced training. The majority of America's teachers have at least a master's degree, according to the NEA.

Teacher licensing and certification programs vary by state, but most fit into the following categories*:

◆ Four- or five-year college degree programs in elementary education or secondary certification, which lead to certification upon graduation.

◆ Post-collegiate programs for college graduates with bachelor's degrees who want to become teachers.

◆ Alternative licensing and certification programs in states where there is a teacher shortage in a particular field. (These programs are typically short-term and intensive to get professionals into the classroom quickly.)

* Source: American Federation of Teachers.

(See Appendix for a description of the requirements to become a certified teacher in six states.)

Chapter 7

The Learning Curve

A few of the students at the New York City elementary school where Donna King used to teach hail from different countries, and they respected her authority because teachers are revered in their cultures. She wonders why teachers in America are not afforded the same level of respect. She also questions why they are not more highly compensated, considering the importance of their jobs. As a parent, she wants her school district to be able to attract highly competent and qualified teachers because they are responsible for her children's educations.

Although salaries for teachers have increased in recent years, "it's never enough," says education professor Linda Barrett. "Teaching is very physically, emotionally and mentally draining, and teachers should be better compensated."

Many jobs are stressful and exhausting. And many jobs are critical to our society and command respect. But do Americans believe these characteristics apply to the teaching profession? Do they feel teachers should be as highly compensated as other professionals who have demanding and vital jobs? One major difference between the teaching profession and most other professions is that the product is children.

All Americans know teachers because they are students, former students or parents. Yet misconceptions about the teaching profession prevail in our society.

Despite the challenges and frustrations they face, many teachers find their jobs rewarding and fulfilling. While the purpose of this book was to convey the difficulties of the teaching profession, there are also many inspirational stories. But not all teachers are altruistic mentors. A series of interviews with parents and administrators would likely produce some stories about inept teachers. In fact, some of the stories in this book are about negative experiences teachers have had with colleagues and administrators. Every profession has its share of incompetence.

But even if parents are displeased with their child's teacher, the child will benefit most if they approach the teacher as a partner. An important message I gleaned from my conversations with teachers is that parents have an important role to play in the school system. Parents have an obligation to participate in their children's educations and a right to advocate for their best interests.

Parents also have the important responsibility of communicating the value of education to their children. Professor Barrett says her biggest issue—which she has emphasized for 30 years—is that parents should prepare their children to respect teachers from the moment they enter the classroom.

While many students are well-behaved and respectful, a few disruptive children can diminish the teacher's focus on academics. Helen Lewis, a teacher in New York City, says she considers her primary responsibility to be the safety of her students, followed by ensuring a sense of decorum in the classroom. Learning ranks third. Children can't learn if they don't feel safe because other chidren are causing them emotional distress or physical harm, she says. A classmate's disruptive behavior also prevents children from learning.

* * *

Confronting the Demands of Teachers

What If Teachers Could Express Their Own Demands?

♦ Students would respect them.

♦ Parents would trust them.

♦ Administrators would support them.

♦ Taxpayers would better compensate them.

* * *

When Kim Thompson tells new acquaintances at social gatherings that she's a teacher, they politely nod and don't inquire further. When Sarah Brown mentions she's a math teacher, the typical response is, "Oh, I hated math." There are no further questions. What I learned from my journey behind the scenes of the American classroom is that all teachers have a story to tell. The question is, are we listening?

Appendix

Certification Requirements for Selected States

ARIZONA

Elementary, K-8 Certification

Provisional Elementary, K-8 Certification

(Provisional certification is valid for two years and is not renewable, but may be extended once for two years.)

- A bachelor's degree or higher from an accredited institution. (Official transcript required.)

- One of the following options:

    (a) Completion of a teacher preparation program in elementary education from an accredited institution or a board-approved teacher preparation program.

    (b) Forty-five semester hours of education courses from an accredited institution including at least eight semester hours of practical application in grades K-8. Two years of verified full-time teaching experience in grades pre-kindergarten-8 may be substituted for the eight semester hours of practical application. (A letter on official letterhead from the district superintendent or personnel director must be submitted to verify teaching experience.)

(c) A valid elementary certificate from another state.

♦ A passing score on the elementary professional knowledge portion of the Arizona Educator Proficiency Assessment (AEPA).

♦ A passing score on the elementary education subject knowledge portion of the Arizona Educator Proficiency Assessment (AEPA).

♦ Verification of state-approved Structured English Immersion (SEI) training. (Individuals with a Full Bilingual or Full ESL endorsement are exempt.)

♦ A photocopy of the individual's valid Arizona Fingerprint Clearance Card issued by the Arizona Department of Public Safety.

♦ Arizona Constitution (a college course or the appropriate examination).

♦ U.S. Constitution (a college course or the appropriate examination).

Note: Individuals who otherwise qualify for the certificate but do not have Arizona and/or U.S. Constitution have three years under a valid teaching certificate to fulfill the requirement, except if they are teaching a course in history, government, social studies, citizenship, law or civics, in which case they have one year to fulfill the requirement.)

Standard Elementary, K-8 Certification

(Standard certification is valid for six years and may be renewed.)

♦ Qualify and hold the Provisional Elementary Certification for two years.

♦ A passing score on the performance portion of the Arizona Educator Proficiency Assessment (AEPA).

◆ Two years of verified full-time teaching experience during the valid period of the provisional certification may be used to convert the Provisional Certificate to a Standard Certificate. (A conversion form signed by the district superintendent or personnel director verifying two years of full-time teaching experience must be submitted.)

◆ Forty-five clock hours or three semester hours of instruction in research-based systematic phonics from an accredited institution or other provider.

◆ Verification of state-approved Structured English Immersion (SEI) training to qualify for a Provisional or Full SEI endorsement. (Individuals with a Full Bilingual or Full ESL endorsement are exempt.)

◆ A photocopy of the individual's Arizona Fingerprint Clearance Card issued by the Arizona Department of Public Safety.

Secondary, 7-12 Certification

Provisional Secondary, 7-12 Certification

(Provisional certification is valid for two years and is not renewable, but may be extended once for two years.)

◆ A bachelor's degree or higher from an accredited institution. (Official transcript required.)

◆ One of the following options:

  (a) Completion of a teacher preparation program in secondary education from an accredited institution or from a board-approved teacher preparation program.

  (b) Thirty semester hours of education courses including at least eight semester hours of practical application in grades 7-12. Two years of verified full-time teaching experience in grades 7 through postsecondary may be substituted for the eight semester hours of practical application. (A letter on official letterhead from the district superintendent or personnel director must be submitted to verify teaching experience.)

(c) A valid secondary certificate from another state.

◆ A passing score on the secondary professional knowledge portion of the Arizona Educator Proficiency Assessment (AEPA).

◆ A passing score on the secondary education subject knowledge portion of the Arizona Educator Proficiency Assessment (AEPA). (If a proficiency assessment is not offered in a subject area, an approved area should consist of a minimum of 24 semester hours of subject-related courses from an accredited institution.)

◆ Verification of state-approved Structured English Immersion (SEI) training. (Individuals who hold a Full Bilingual or Full ESL endorsement are exempt.)

◆ A photocopy of the individual's valid Arizona Fingerprint Clearance Card issued by the Arizona Department of Public safety.

◆ Arizona Constitution (a college course or the appropriate examination).

◆ U.S. Constitution (a college course or the appropriate examination).

Note: Individuals who otherwise qualify for the certificate but do not have Arizona and/or U.S. Constitution have three years under a valid teaching certificate to fulfill the requirement, except if they are teaching a course in history, government, social studies, citizenship, law or civics, in which case they have one year to fulfill the requirement.)

Standard Secondary, 7-12 Certification
(Standard certification is valid for six years and may be renewed.)

◆ Qualify and hold the Provisional Elementary Certification for two years.

◆ A passing score on the performance portion of the Arizona Educator Proficiency Assessment (AEPA).

◆ Two years of verified full-time teaching experience during the valid period of the provisional certification may be used to convert the Provisional Certificate to a Standard Certificate. (A conversion form signed by the district superintendent or personnel director verifying two years of full-time teaching experience must be submitted.)

◆ Verification of state-approved Structured English Immersion (SEI) training to qualify for a Provisional or Full SEI endorsement. (Individuals with Full Bilingual or Full ESL endorsement are exempt.)

◆ A photocopy of the individual's Arizona Fingerprint Clearance Card issued by the Arizona Department of Public Safety.

Certification Renewal Requirements

◆ District verification of professional development training.

◆ An official transcript of academic coursework completed during the valid period of the certificate to be renewed from an accredited institution.

Source: Arizona Department of Education

CALIFORNIA

Multiple Subject Teaching Credential

(Individuals who want to teach elementary school in California are required to earn a Multiple Subject Teaching Credential.)

Preliminary Credential

(The Preliminary Credential is issued for a maximum of five years. If requirements for the Clear Credential are not completed before the expiration of the preliminary, the holder will be unable to teach in California's public schools until those requirements are met.)

◆ Complete a baccalaureate or higher degree, except in professional education, from a regionally accredited college or university.

◆ Satisfy the basic skills requirement by one of the following methods:

(a) Pass the CBEST.

(b) Pass the CSET.

(c) Pass a basic skills exam from another state.

◆ Complete a multiple subject teacher preparation program, including successful student-teaching, and obtain a formal recommendation for the credential from the California college or university where the program was completed.

◆ Verify subject matter competence by one of the following methods:

(a) Achieve a passing score on the appropriate subject matter exams.

(b) Complete a commission-approved elementary subject matter program or its equivalent and obtain verification of completion from the authorized person in the education department of a California college or university with an accredited program. (This option is available only to those individuals who completed the subject matter program and enrolled in a teacher preparation program prior to July 1, 2004.)

◆ Pass the Reading Instruction Competence Assessment. (Individuals who hold valid California teaching credentials that were issued based upon completion of a teacher preparation program including student-teaching are exempt from this requirement.)

◆ Satisfy the Developing English Language Skills, including Reading, requirement by completing a comprehensive reading instruction course that includes the following: systematic study of phonemic awareness, phonics and decoding; literature, language and comprehension; and diagnostic and early intervention techniques.

- Complete a course in the provisions and principles of the U.S. Constitution or pass an exam given by a regionally accredited college or university.

- Complete foundational computer technology course work that includes general and specialized skills in the use of computers in educational settings.

Clear Credential

Individuals who complete a teacher preparation program and receive a five-year preliminary credential must earn a clear credential by satisfying one of the following three options:

(a) Complete a commission-approved Professional Teacher Induction Program through an approved school district county office of education, college or university, consortium or private school. The indication program includes the advanced study of health education, special populations, computer technology, and teaching English learners.

(b) Complete a commission-approved fifth year of study at a California college or university, securing that institution's formal recommendation for the clear credential. (This option is available only to holders of Preliminary Credentials issued before August 30, 2004.) The following must be verified with the application for the clear credential:

- Advanced course work in health education that includes nutrition; the physiological and sociological effects of alcohol, narcotics, and drug abuse; and the use of tobacco.

- Advanced course work in the laws, methods and requirements for providing educational opportunities to special populations in the regular classroom.

- Advanced course work in computer technology, including the use of computers in education settings.

◆ Advanced course work in teaching English learners.

(c) Teachers who are certified by the National Board of Professional Teaching Standards in Early Childhood (ages 3-8)/Generalist or Middle Childhood (ages 7-12)/Generalist will be issued a Clear Multiple Subject Teaching Credential.

Single Subject Teaching Credential

(Individuals who want to teach middle school and high school in California are required to earn a Single Subject Teaching Credential.)

Preliminary Credential

(The Preliminary Credential is issued for a maximum of five years. If requirements for the Clear Credential are not completed before the expiration of the preliminary, the holder will be unable to teach in California's public schools until those requirements are met.)

◆ Complete a baccalaureate or higher degree, except in professional education, from a regionally accredited college or university.

◆ Satisfy the basic skills requirement by one of the following methods:

(a) Pass the CBEST.

(b) Pass the CSET.

(c) Pass a basic skills exam from another state.

◆ Complete a single subject teacher preparation program, including successful student-teaching, and obtain a formal recommendation for the credential from the California college or university where the program was completed.

◆ Verify subject matter competence by one of the following methods:

(a) Achieve a passing score on the appropriate subject matter exams.

(b) Complete a commission-approved subject-matter program or its equivalent and obtain verification of completion from the authorized person in the education department of a California college or university with an accredited program.

(c) For Specialized Science subjects only, individuals may take and pass the appropriate subject matter exams or obtain verification of completion of subject matter course work from the Commission on Teacher Credentialing.

◆ Satisfy the Developing English Language Skills, including Reading, requirement by completing a comprehensive reading instruction course that includes the following: systematic study of phonemic awareness, phonics and decoding; literature, language and comprehension; and diagnostic and early intervention techniques.

◆ Complete a course in the provisions and principles of the U.S. Constitution or pass an exam given by a regionally accredited college or university.

◆ Complete foundational computer technology course work that includes general and specialized skills in the use of computers in educational settings.

Clear Credential

Individuals who complete a teacher preparation program and receive a five-year preliminary credential must earn a clear credential by satisfying one of the following three options:

(a) Complete a commission-approved Professional Teacher Induction Program through an approved school district county office of education, college or university, consortium or private school. The indication program includes the advanced study of health education, special populations, computer technology, and teaching English learners.

(b) Complete a commission-approved fifth year of study completed at a California college or university, securing that institution's formal recommendation for the clear credential. (This option is available only to holders of Preliminary Credentials issued before August 30, 2004.) The following must be verified with the application for the clear credential:

- ◆ Advanced course work in health education that includes nutrition, the physiological and sociological effects of alcohol, narcotics, and drug abuse; and the use of tobacco.

- ◆ Advanced course work in the laws, methods and requirements for providing educational opportunities to special populations in the regular classroom.

- ◆ Advanced course work in computer technology, including the use of computers in education settings.

- ◆ Advanced course work in teaching English learners.

(c) Teachers who are certified by the National Board of Professional Teaching Standards will be issued a Clear Teaching Credential in the subject area in which they have received national certification.

Source: California Commission on Teacher Credentialing

FLORIDA

Temporary Certification

(The Temporary Certificate is valid for three years and may not be renewed.)

- ◆ A bachelor's degree or higher from an accredited or approved institution.

- ◆ Demonstrate mastery of subject area knowledge.

- ◆ Complete the degree or course requirements outlined in Florida State Board of Education Rules for the subject the individual requests with a GPA of 2.5 in the subject courses.

Professional Credential

(The Professional Certificate is valid for five years and may be renewed.)

- A bachelor's degree or higher from an accredited or approved institution.

- Demonstrate mastery of general knowledge by one of the following options:

    (a) Achievement of a passing score on the Florida General Knowledge Test.

    (b) Achievement of a passing score on the Florida College Level Academic Skills Test (CLAST) earned prior to July 1, 2002.

    (c) A valid standard teaching certificate issued by another U.S. state, U.S. territory, National Board of Professional Teaching Standards or American Board for Certification of Teacher Excellence.

    (d) Two semesters of full-time college teaching experience at an accredited or approved institution.

- Demonstrate mastery of subject area knowledge by satisfying one of the following requirements:

    (a) For bachelor's degree level subjects, achievement of a passing score on the appropriate Florida subject area exam earned after July 1, 2002.

    (b) For master's degree level subjects, completion of the required degree and content courses listed in the State Board Rule for the subject and achievement of passing score on the appropriate Florida subject area exam.

    (c) For all subject areas, a valid standard certificate issued in the subject at the same degree level required in Florida by another U.S. state, U.S. territory, National Board of Professional Teaching Standards or American Board for Certification of Teacher Excellence.

◆ Demonstrate mastery of professional preparation and education competence by satisfying one of the following requirements:

(a) Completion of a state-approved teaching preparation program or a teacher education program from an institution outside Florida and achievement of a passing score on the Florida Professional Education Test.

(b) A valid standard certificate issued by another U.S. state, U.S. territory or National Board of Professional Teaching Standards.

(c) A valid standard certificate issued by the American Board for Certification of Teacher Excellence and completion of an approved professional education competence demonstration system.

(d) Completion of a state-approved alternative certification program.

(e) Completion of 20 semester hours of specified education courses, completion of an approved professional education competence demonstration system, and achievement of a passing score on the Florida Professional Education Test.

(f) Two semesters of full-time college teaching experience at an accredited or approved institution.

Certification Renewal Requirements

◆ Six semester hours of college credit or the equivalent must be earned during each renewal period at an accredited or approved institution.

Source: Florida Department of Education

MICHIGAN

Provisional Certificate (initial) (in-state candidates)

◆ Successful completion of an approved Michigan teacher preparation program.

◆ The certificate is valid for up to six years, during which the individual is expected to gain experience as a successful practicing professional and to acquire additional professional development through advance study (completion of at least 18 semester hours in a planned course of study) as a prerequisite for the next level of certification.

◆ The certificate can be renewed for up to three years with the completion of 10 semester credit hours in a planned program at an approved teacher preparation institution.

◆ A second three-year renewal requires completion of 18 semester hours in a planned program at an approved teacher preparation institution.

Professional Education Certificate (advanced) (in-state candidates)

(The professional education certificate is valid for up to five years.)

◆ Completion of 18 semester hours in a planned course of study after the issuance of the Provisional Certificate.

◆ Completion of Michigan's reading requirement (six semester hours of teaching reading for elementary teachers or three semester hours for secondary teachers).

◆ Three years of successful teaching experience.

Source: Michigan Department of Education

NEW YORK

(Following are certification requirements for a selected sample of three subject areas/grade levels.)

Childhood Education (Grades 1-6)

(Following are the requirements for individuals who pursue certification through an approved teacher preparation program.)

Initial Certificate

(The initial certificate is valid for five years.)

◆ Completion of a New York State registered program—Childhood Education (Grades 1-6)

◆ Institutional recommendation

◆ New York State Teacher Certification Exam—Liberal Arts & Science Test

◆ New York State Teacher Certification Exam—Elementary Assessment of Teaching Skills

◆ Content Specialty Test—Multi-Subject

◆ Fingerprint clearance

Professional Certificate

(Continuously valid with the completion of required professional development hours on a five-year professional development cycle.)

◆ Completion of a New York State registered program—Childhood Education (Grades 1-6)

◆ Institutional Recommendation

◆ New York State Teacher Certification Exam—Liberal Arts & Science Test

◆ New York State Teacher Certification Exam—Elementary Assessment of Teaching Skills

◆ Content Specialty Test—Multi-Subject

◆ Paid, full-time classroom teaching experience for three years

◆ Mentored experience for one year

◆ Fingerprint clearance

◆ Citizenship status

Middle Childhood Education/Generalist (Grades 5-9)

(Following are the requirements for individuals who pursue certification through an approved teacher preparation program.)

Initial Certification

(Initial certification is valid for five years.)

- Completion of a New York State registered program—Generalist in Middle Childhood Education (Grades 5-9)

- Institutional recommendation

- New York State Teacher Certification Exam—Liberal Arts & Science Test

- New York State Teacher Certification Exam—Secondary Assessment of Teaching Skills

- Content Specialty Test—Multi-Subject

- Fingerprint clearance

Professional Certificate

(Continuously valid with the completion of required professional development hours on a five-year professional development cycle.)

- Completion of a New York State registered program—Generalist in Middle Childhood Education (Grades 5-9)

- Institutional Recommendation

- New York State Teacher Certification Exam—Liberal Arts & Science Test

- New York State Teacher Certification Exam—Secondary Assessment of Teaching Skills

- Content Specialty Test—Multi-Subject

- Paid, full-time classroom teaching experience for three years

- Mentored experience for one year

- Fingerprint clearance
- Citizenship status

English Language Arts (Grades 7-12)

(Following are the requirements for individuals who pursue certification through an approved teacher preparation program.)

Initial Certification

(Initial certification is valid for five years.)

- Completion of a New York State registered program—English Language Arts (Grades 7-12)
- Institutional recommendation
- New York State Teacher Certification Exam—Liberal Arts & Science Test
- New York State Teacher Certification Exam—Secondary Assessment of Teaching Skills
- Content Specialty Test—English Language Arts
- Fingerprint clearance

Professional Certificate

(Continuously valid with the completion of required professional development hours on a five-year professional development cycle.)

- Completion of a New York State registered program—English Language Arts (Grades 7-12)
- Institutional Recommendation
- New York State Teacher Certification Exam—Liberal Arts & Science Test
- New York State Teacher Certification Exam—Secondary Assessment of Teaching Skills

- Content Specialty Test—English Language Arts
- Paid, full-time classroom teaching experience for three years
- Mentored experience for one year
- Fingerprint clearance
- Citizenship status

Source: New York State Education Department

TEXAS

Standard Certification

(Standard Certification is valid for five years.)

- Earn a bachelor's degree from an accredited college or university. (Texas institutions do not offer degrees in education. Teachers must have an academic major and teacher training courses.)

- Complete teacher training through an approved program. (Programs are offered through colleges and universities, school districts, regional service centers, community colleges, and other entities.)

- Successfully complete the appropriate teacher certification tests for the subject and grade level desired.

Certification Renewal Requirements

- Classroom teachers must complete 150 clock hours of continuing professional education (CPE) during the renewal period through the following:

    (a) Workshops, conferences, and in-service or staff development delivered by an approved registered provider.

    (b) Undergraduate and graduate coursework through an accredited institution of higher education with one semester credit being equivalent to 15 CPE clock hours.

(c) Interactive distance learning, video conferencing or online activities.

(d) Independent study, not to exceed 20% of the required clock hours.

(e) Development of curriculum or CPE training materials.

(f) Presenting CPE activities, not to exceed 10% of the required clock hours.

(g) Serving as a mentor, not to exceed 30% of the required clock hours.

(h) Serving as an assessor for the principal assessment, not to exceed 10% of the required clock hours.

Source: Texas State Board for Educator Certification

Bibliography

Chapter 2: The Classroom Management Struggle

Substance Abuse and Mental Health Services Administration, United States Department of Health and Human Services. "The Myth of the Bad Kid." http://mentalhealth.samhsa.gov/publications/allpubs/Ca-0021/default.asp (accessed October 21, 2007).

Substance Abuse and Mental Health Services Administration, United States Department of Health and Human Services. "Children's Mental Health Facts. Children and Adolescents with Mental, Emotional, and Behavioral Disorders." http://mentalhealth.samhsa.gov/publications/allpubs/CA-0006/default.asp (accessed October 21, 2007).

Anxiety Disorders Association of America. "Anxiety Disorders in Children and Teens." http://www.adaa.org/GettingHelp/FocusOn/Children&Adolescents.asp (accessed October 21, 2007).

National Institute of Mental Health, National Institutes of Health, United States Department of Health and Human

Services. "Attention Deficit Hyperactivity Disorder."
http://www.nimh.nih.gov/health/publications/adhd/complete-publication.shtml (accessed October 21, 2007).

American Academy of Child & Adolescent Psychiatry. "Child and Adolescent Mental Illness and Drug Abuse Statistics." http://www.aacap.org/cs/root/resources_for_families/child_and_adolescent_mental_illness_statistics (accessed October 21, 2007).

United States Department of Education. "New Study Shows Smaller Classes Enhance Academic Achievement." http://www.ed.gov/PressReleases/05-1998/doverd.html. (accessed April 3, 2008).

American Educational Research Association. "Class Size: Counting Students CanCount." http://www.aera.net/uploadedFiles/Journals_and_Publications/Research_Points/RP_Fall03.pdf (accessed April 3, 2008).

Chapter 3: Parents—Allies or Adversaries

Wikipedia. "Helicopter parent." http://en.wikipedia.org/wiki/Helicopter_parent (accessed October 20, 2007).

Dillon, Sam. "A Great Year for Ivy League Schools, but Not So Good for Applicants to Them." *The New York Times*, April 4, 2007.

Arenson, Karen W. "Applications to Colleges Are Breaking Records." *The New York Times*, January 17, 2008.

National Parent Teacher Association (PTA). "National Standards for Family-School Partnerships." http://pta.org/documents/National_Standards.pdf (accessed February 22, 2008).

Chapter 4: Office Politics

National Education Association (NEA). "NEA Examines the Rights of Nontenured Teachers." http://www.nea.org/neatoday/0105/rights.html (accessed November 5, 2007).

United States Department of Education. "The No Child Left Behind Act of 2001." http://www.ed.gov/nclb/overview/intro/execsumm.doc (accessed November 5, 2007).

United States Department of Education. "Facts and Terms Every Parent Should Know About NCLB." http://www.ed.gov/nclb/overview/intro/parents/parentfacts.html (accessed November 5, 2007).

Chapter 5: Occupational Hazards

American Academy of Child & Adolescent Psychiatry. "Glossary of Symptoms and Mental Illnesses Affecting Teenagers." http://www.aacap.org/cs/root/resources_for_families/glossary_of_ symptoms_and_mental_illnesses_affecting_teenagers (accessed October 21, 2007).

Administration for Children & Families, United States Department of Health & Human Services. "Summary, Child Maltreatment 2005." http://www.acf.dhhs.gov/programs/cb/pubs/cm05/summary.htm (accessed October 21, 2007).

United States Census Bureau, Housing and Household Economic Statistics Division. "Poverty: 2006 Highlights." http://www.census.gov/hhes/www/poverty/poverty06/pov06hi.html (accessed October 21, 2007).

United States Department of Education; United States Department of Justice. "Indicators of School Crime and Safety, 2007." http://nces.ed.gov/pubsearch/pubsinfo.asp?pubid=2007003 (accessed October 21, 2007).

Chapter 6: The Truth About the 9-to-3 Job

National Education Association (NEA). "National Teacher Day Spotlights Key Issues Facing Profession," May 2, 2006.

http://www.nea.org/newsreleases/2006/nr060502.html
(accessed October 21, 2007).

The United Federation of Teachers (UFT). "Teacher Resignations
Hit Record High," November 19, 2007. http://www.uft.org/news/
issues/press/teacher_resignations (accessed November 26, 2007).

National Education Association (NEA). "Professional Pay,
Myths and Facts." http://nea.org/pay/teachermyths.html
(accessed March 2, 2007).

United States Department of Labor, Bureau of Labor Statistics.
"May 2006 National Occupational Employment and Wage
Estimates." http://stats.bls.gov/oes/current/oes_nat.htm
(accessed January 1, 2008).

National Education Association (NEA). "Teacher Salary Lags
Behind Inflation," December 10, 2007. http://www.nea.org/news
releases/2007/nr071210.html (accessed January 1, 2008).

American Federation of Teachers (AFT). "AFT Salary Survey:
Teachers Need 30 Percent Raise; Teacher Pay Insufficient to Meet
Rising Debt, Housing Costs in Many Areas," March 29, 2007.
http://www.aft.org/presscenter/releases/2007/032907.htm (accessed
October 21, 2007).

National Education Association (NEA). "Too Many Children
Losing Good Teachers," June 19, 2007. http://www.nea.org/news
releases/2007/nr070619.html (accessed October 21, 2007).

American Federation of Teachers (AFT). "Becoming a Teacher."
http://www.aft.org/teachers/jft/becoming.htm (accessed
November 5, 2007).

Appendix

Arizona Department of Education. "Arizona Teacher Certification."

http://ade.state.az.us/certification (accessed December 30, 2007).

California Commission on Teacher Credentialing. "Become a Teacher in California." http://www.ctc.ca.gov/credentials/teach.html (accessed December 30, 2007).

Florida Department of Education. "Educator Certification." http://www.fldoe.org/edcert (accessed December 30, 2007).

Michigan Department of Education. "Michigan Teacher Certification for In-State Candidates." http://www.michigan.gov/mde (accessed December 30, 2007).

New York State Education Department, Office of Teaching Initiatives. "Search Certification Requirements." http://eservices.nysed.gov/teach/certhelp (accessed December 30, 2007).

Texas State Board for Educator Certification. "How to Become a Teacher in Texas." http://www.sbec.state.tx.us/SBECOnline/certinfo/becometeacher.asp (accessed December 30, 2007).

Acknowledgments

About a year ago, I was having dinner with a friend, and she mentioned she used to be a teacher. A devastating incident prompted her to pursue a new career. A parent entered her classroom and physically attacked her. Her story shocked me, and several days later it remained on my mind. It conjured up a memory of a conversation I had at a party a few years earlier. A woman was complaining about her school taxes, griping that teachers were paid too much because they worked until 3 o'clock and enjoyed summers off. I thought about the teachers I knew and the stories they had told me about the day-to-day stresses, underlying politics and anxiety-producing aspects of their profession. I thought about the discrepancy between society's perception of the teaching profession and the actual experience. My ruminations eventually led me to conceive of the idea for this book. I am grateful to my friend for sharing her story, which ultimately inspired me to write *The Teacher Chronicles*.

Thank you to all of the teachers who made this book possible by graciously agreeing to tell me your stories. I am deeply grateful for your cooperation and support.

Thank you to my friends and family (and their friends and family) for diligently and enthusiastically recruiting teachers for me to interview.

Thank you to my friends, family and colleagues who read my manuscript and provided insightful feedback.

Thank you to my family for your support, guidance and encouragement throughout this project.

Thank you to my teachers. I still remember each one of you and the impact you made on my life.

About the Author

Natalie Schwartz is a freelance writer and editor based in New York. She previously served as managing editor at Corporate Research Group in New Rochelle, New York. Prior to joining Corporate Research Group, she held a managing editor position at Simba Information in Stamford, Connecticut. She was a reporter with a local newspaper in Westchester County, New York, before joining Simba. She is an active volunteer with the PTA (Parent Teacher Association) in her local school district. She graduated in 1991 from Cornell University with a bachelor's degree in communication.